Pr

ReThink Resilience

"This is a second must-read book from Beth Kennedy. It's an extension of her brilliant resilience model fortified with testimonials and real-life examples. This book is written in co-authorship with two brilliant biopharma scientists, Ben and Karthik, who continue contributing to the well-being of the scientific community. I can't wait to see this book in print. I plan to keep it on my desk and read one booster a day, savoring it and reflecting upon it."

—Elena Izmailova, PhD, Chief Scientific Officer, Koneksa Health

"In the world of work—and in the world—we all need strategies to build or maintain our resilience. In *ReThink Resilience: 99 Ways to ReCharge Your Career and Life*, everyone can find something that will resonate with and work for them! The authors have compiled an extensive list of strategies, organized by the Benatti Resiliency Model®, which provides an understanding of the factors of resilience. My personal favorites so far are 'Play Tourist Where You Live,' as I have moved to a new part of the country; 'Approach AI with Curiosity,' because we all should; and 'Introduce Yourself with Your Brand,' as I have always emphasized the importance of being intentional about how you want to be known.

You'll find very practical tactics and techniques to firm up your resilience in this book—pick a few and see the impact!"

—Eileen Habelow, PhD, Founder and President, Leadership-Link

"Resilience defines my career and life for that matter. It is where grit and persistence establish a 'groove.' Beth and her co-authors promote this ideology in a thought-provoking way!"

—Art Johnson, author of *The Art of Alignment*; Founder, Infinity Systems, Inc.

"As a client of Beth's for over twenty-five years through different industries, companies, and roles, I am thrilled that she is sharing her knowledge and experience with a broader audience with the publication of *ReThink Resilience*. After experiencing burnout in my former position, Beth helped me recover and recharge through her resilience strategies, leading me from bitter and broken semiretirement to engaged and fulfilled full-time contributor. In her new book, Beth and her co-authors have distilled her positive, affirming approach into a unique resource that everyone can use."

—Elliot Schwartz, PhD, Performance Innovation Lead, US Olympic & Paralympic Committee

"*ReThink Resilience* is an easy read and an excellent reminder of how being intentional about making small changes in our lives can make an enormous difference—both personally and professionally. It is a must-read for those who want to avoid burnout, revive, or build and preserve their resilience."

—Angie Bado, President, Public Schools First McKinney

"*ReThink Resilience* offers a transformative approach to building resilience in both personal and professional life. Combining their extensive experience and research, the authors provide practical strategies and actionable insights to enhance well-being, self-awareness, brand development, connection, and innovation. Perfect for anyone seeking to boost their resilience, this book is a valuable resource for fostering growth and fulfillment."

—**Marshall Goldsmith,** Thinkers50 #1 Executive Coach and *New York Times* best-selling author of *The Earned Life*, *Triggers*, and *What Got You Here Won't Get You There*

"Beth and her co-authors share hard-won wisdom in very relatable, short chunks filled with practical suggestions that even the most experienced professionals can benefit from implementing! Taking on even a few of the possible approaches will certainly nurture resilience as change swirls all around us."

—**Dr. Deborah Dunsire,** Chairperson, Neurvati Neurosciences; Former CEO, H. Lundbeck A/S

"*ReThink Resilience* offers a straightforward approach to refreshing, restarting, and invigorating your mindset toward work and personal well-being. Packed with easy-to-implement tips and tricks, this book guides you through building resilience across five key areas, with a personal favorite on the importance of building connections, making it a valuable resource for anyone looking to strengthen their resilience and enhance their life."

—**Karen Casey,** Chief People Officer, Syner-G BioPharma Group

ReThink Resilience

99 Ways

to ReCharge Your Career and Life

BETH BENATTI KENNEDY, MS, LMFT

KARTHIK VENKATAKRISHNAN, PhD, FCP

SONGMAO (BEN) ZHENG, PhD

RIVER GROVE
BOOKS

Published by River Grove Books
Austin, TX
www.rivergrovebooks.com

Distributed by River Grove Books

Design and composition by Greenleaf Book Group
Cover design by Greenleaf Book Group
Cover Image: RemoNonaz/shutterstock.com

Publisher's Cataloging-in-Publication data is available.

Print ISBN: 978-1-63299-841-5

eBook ISBN: 978-1-63299-842-2

First Edition

Gratitude

I want to express my heartfelt gratitude to my mother, Joan W. Benatti, and my mother-in-law, Jeanne C. Kennedy. Both of them have exemplified resilience and the art of recharging over many years. Their unwavering strength and positive outlook have been a source of inspiration for me. I am fortunate to continue learning from their wisdom and experiences.

—Beth Benatti Kennedy

I am grateful to my mother, Shantha Venkatakrishnan, and my father, K. A. Venkatakrishnan, for their unwavering love and trust. My mother, a scientist and literary scholar, inspired me to embrace science as an art. Earlier this year, she published a beautiful book of soulful poems. I am honored to follow her lead with my contribution to *ReThink Resilience*, reinforcing my gratitude and celebrating our shared path.

—Karthik Venkatakrishnan

I want to dedicate this book to my mother, Hui Li, my father, Jinchuan Zheng, and my husband, Brent Hackett. They have nurtured and shaped me in remarkable ways, taught me valuable lessons, and loved me for who I am. I am grateful to be part of their life journeys, to witness and to learn from their perseverance, resourcefulness, agility, and resilience.

—Songmao (Ben) Zheng

Contents

About the Cover

The cover image is an artist-rendered illustration of the iconic Longfellow Bridge that connects Boston to Cambridge, going across the Charles River against an often-dramatic silhouette of blue or gray skies that inspire Well-being and Self-awareness. Bridges, with their powerful Brand, represent resilience, especially when set against an impressive skyline that evokes potential, hope, and untold stories. The bridge serves as a conduit for the exchange of ideas across sectors in the Greater Boston area such as academic, professional, and social communities, nurturing Connection and Innovation.

Acknowledgments

Our thanks to our book project manager, Melissa Corcoran. Her attention to detail, coupled with her caring and commitment, ensured that every aspect of this book was handled with utmost precision. She coordinated countless elements, edited our diverse writing styles into a cohesive whole, and transformed our vision into a reality. We are deeply grateful for her invaluable contribution and dedication.

When writing this book, we asked people who modeled resilience to talk about it with us. Our thanks to Lisa J. Benincosa, Chen Chen, Edna F. Choo, Melissa Corcoran, Gayle Draper, Neeraj Gupta, Brent A. Hackett, Michael J. Hanley, Donald Heald, John Kelley, Parag Mallick, Ashley Milton, Erik Modahl, Deborah Nguyen, Sharon J. Swan, and

Alexandra S. Zappala for their generous participation. Their insights and stories add immeasurably to the book and are examples of resilience in action. We are delighted to present a word cloud that encapsulates the words of wisdom of our Resilience Champions.

Introduction

I f you are successful, you might equate that with being resilient; many people think that as long as they are able to keep going, they are resilient. But being resilient does not mean you put your head down and power through. Being resilient means you have the skills to handle change and to recover and recharge yourself so you have the energy needed for a productive, engaging career and life.

The cornerstone of this book is the Benatti Resiliency Model®. The model was developed by Beth Benatti Kennedy several years ago after she coached employees at all levels of an organization that had been acquired by another company. She observed that individuals with career resilience were able to drive their careers, make the choice to not let the acquisition "ruin their lives," and find opportunities even in a challenging situation. Beth identified five strategies that these people possessed as part of their career toolbox, which became her Benatti Resiliency Model. Not only did Beth incorporate these strategies into her leadership coaching and training practice, she also turned them into her first book, *Career ReCharge: Five Strategies to Boost Resilience and Beat Burnout.*

Dr. Karthik Venkatakrishnan is a past mentee of Beth's and credits their work together for enabling his successful transition from a scientific leadership role to a global strategic leadership role in the pharmaceutical industry sector. Through Beth's coaching and his mindful practice of the five strategies of the Benatti Resiliency Model, including defining and nurturing his professional brand, Karthik was able to make this transition without losing his authentic, brand-defining approach to people-focused and science-driven leadership. Appreciating the importance of resilience as a key leadership competency and aware of the lack of broader awareness of these principles in the biomedical and pharmaceutical research and development sector, Karthik and Beth collaborated to open the eyes of these communities of practice by writing a commentary that was published in *Clinical and Translational Science,* a peer-reviewed journal of the American Society for Clinical Pharmacology and Therapeutics. This publication established a valuable collaboration between the two authors, which then led to opportunities to continue research on this topic, especially as the world grappled with the COVID-19 pandemic.

Karthik introduced Beth to Dr. Songmao (Ben) Zheng, a scientific leader in the (bio)pharmaceutical industry, whom

Karthik had previously known through professional organization engagement. The three authors joined forces on a scientific journal publication integrating more than a year's research surveying the practice of resilience among professionals in 2021 and further identifying strategies to boost resilience and prevent burnout. This research was published in *Clinical and Translational Science* in 2022, continuing the journey of raising awareness of opportunities to enhance resilience as a key leadership competency.

Energized by their successful collaborations, the three authors decided to write this book for the reader who is unable to dedicate the time and commitment required to read an in-depth book on resilience. The resilience boosters you'll find here are practical and bite-sized and can be readily integrated into your work and life. You can read them in any order, picking out whichever ones resonate with you. Since each booster is categorized by one or more strategies of the Benatti Resiliency Model, you can also select boosters that pertain to a specific strategy. Also included are insights from sixteen "Resilience Champions," people personally known to the authors who model resilience.

We realize that not everyone will be able to practice every booster. Being resilient is like going on a trip, the itinerary for which is different for everyone. Our wish is for you to practice resilience and develop habits that will impact and influence your career and life, enabling professional success and personal fulfillment.

The Benatti Resiliency Model®

There are five strategies of the Benatti Resiliency Model:

- Well-being: physical, emotional, and spiritual health

- Self-awareness: purpose, mindset, and personality type

- Brand: attributes, impact, and reputation

- Connection: cultivating relationships

- Innovation: challenging yourself

Well-being is about exercise, nutrition, sleep, dealing with stressors, making opportunities for fun, and relaxation—all these factors can be a wellspring of energy if paid attention to and are key to being productive and focused.

Self-awareness includes purpose, mindset, and personality type. Your purpose defines the direction in which you would like to see your career and life move. Having the mindset that you have control over your personal and professional achievements helps you move forward. Knowing the natural gifts and challenges of your personality type is key to functioning well in the workplace.

Do you know what your **brand** is? Brand isn't just the attributes that describe you—for example, strategic, detail-oriented, collaborative—it's also about the impact you make in your position. It doesn't just differentiate you in the marketplace; knowing your brand also lets you be more visible and proactive in your career. It is vital to communicate your brand in an authentic manner through visual, verbal, and behavioral cues, as well as online.

Connection is your support system; strong relationships are the strongest predictor of life and career satisfaction. Connection is *not* about gathering as many business cards and social media connections as possible but is about creating and nourishing trusting relationships in your professional and personal life.

Focusing on **innovation** keeps you growing, flexible, and thinking creatively and avoids burnout. What are you doing in the next three months to challenge yourself, to learn something new and innovative? It can be career-related, a new hobby or interest you have decided to bring into your life, attending a class, or as simple as reading a book or blog that is relevant to your field.

One way to start your journey to resilience is to benchmark it at https://bethkennedy.com/rethink-resilience-benchmark/.

Photograph of the authors taken on November 12, 2022, after the five-hour kick-off meeting in Boston that initiated the journey of writing this book. (Left to right: Songmao [Ben] Zheng, Beth Benatti Kennedy, Karthik Venkatakrishnan)

1

Adjust your computer screen to protect your eyes.

Well-being

When you work with computer screens all day long, they can be a stressor. Factors such as brightness and screen colors do matter, as well as getting a monitor that fits your purpose and preference. One option is to use eye-protection colors (e.g., *Hue = 84, Saturation = 86, Luminosity = 215* or *Red = 219, Green = 238, Blue = 221*). Give it a try and see if it works for you.

2

Appreciate and learn from animals even if you don't have one.

Well-being, Self-awareness, Connection

A nimals are smarter than we often give them credit for and can teach us life lessons beneficial to our overall well-being, happiness, and resilience. Look for animal-focused programs on TV, YouTube, or a streaming service—they may cast light on what you don't know you don't know. Be kind and patient to your pets if you have one or to your neighbors' pets if you don't. Think about what they have done for us, and we shall do the same for them! After all, the earth is to be shared by all living creatures, not just humans.

Beth's golden retriever Maple—office mate and recharge partner.

3

Ask for help.

Well-being, Connection

Asking for help is a strength, not a weakness. Nurture and build your resilience by reaching out to a loving family member, a close friend, a trustworthy colleague, an understanding mentor, or a professional therapist when facing a challenge that cannot be readily resolved by yourself. Don't be afraid of speaking up about your concerns and frustrations. Talking to someone in your support system can provide empathy and a sounding board, shift your perspective, and remind you that you are not alone in your challenge or helpless when removing a roadblock. In addition, asking for help fosters stronger relationships and connections and enables greater awareness on your end of what others may need.

4

Be mindful in designing
your living space.

Well-being, Innovation

The ambience you live in influences your well-being, happiness, and productivity. Light, sound, nature, and art are some dimensions to consider when designing your living space. Careful selection of window treatments, warm-colored light bulbs, and layered lighting with lamps and dimmer switches are some strategies to maximize the way light exposure and its modulation can be optimized depending on the time of day and the activities of daily living.

Sound is an equally important component to manage and may require active investment in noise neutralization (e.g., from city traffic) while inviting certain sounds (e.g., nature, relaxing music) at the right times to help channel positive energy flow. Together with plants, wall art, and other interior decorations, the overall design of your living space can contribute to a positive mindset.

If working from home, place your desk close to a window to benefit from the sunlight and view of the outdoors once in a while. Set boundaries that separate your workspace from living space, even if they are physically part of an open layout.

Equally important is to avoid hoarding, minimize clutter, and dedicate time for regular cleaning and maintaining of your living space.

5

Breathing is magic.

Well-being

We cannot survive without breathing, but breathing properly is underemphasized and underappreciated for its immense functionality and benefits. It can help rid the lungs of accumulated stale air, increase oxygen levels, and get the diaphragm to return to its job of helping you breathe. It may also decrease stress, increase calmness, and alleviate pain. Try doing a pause breath throughout your day, perhaps before a meeting or when you are feeling tired.

Take one mindful breath to reset and calm your body and mind in less than six seconds. For the most relaxing results, breathe through your diaphragm and expand the belly for a count of four, hold for two, and then exhale completely for six. Repeat three times.

Breathe through your diaphragm and expand the belly for a count of four.

Hold for two.

Exhale completely for six.

Repeat three times.

6

Capture vivid memories via pictures.

Well-being, Self-awareness, Innovation

Scientific evidence has suggested that the neurological retrieval of happiness can come from vivid memories, and photography is one way to capture those memories. The best camera is the one you carry with you on a daily basis, so explore photography with the camera you have—that is, your phone! Don't feel pressured if your photos are not the same as those on social media or as those from professional photographers—photography is a very personal endeavor. Conversely, there is no need to take photos for the sake of taking photos. Sometimes, being in the moment and immersing yourself in the experience is all that is needed.

Overleaf: photos taken with cell phones by Beth, Karthik, and Songmao.

Words on resilience from Resilience Champion Deborah Nguyen

I have dealt with chronic pain my whole life. My migraines started in elementary school, and as an adult I was diagnosed with fibromyalgia. In college, I started each day with two Excedrin and an aspirin, kept in my bedside table because I couldn't fathom having to go all the way to the medicine cabinet. Sometimes I had to go to the emergency room to treat my pain. Newer therapies have helped immensely across time, but even now I have days where I spend the first couple of hours getting myself functional. I've still been able to achieve a PhD and a successful career in industry.

Treating my pain likely impacted my ability to start a family as well, but I was able to make my desire to have a family a reality through adoption. Throughout these challenges, I've developed considerable resilience—when times are tough, I keep my eyes on the next steps that are in line with my deepest values, identify what I can control, and take those steps forward. I can't always see where the finish line is, but I know if I keep showing up, I will find my way through.

A resilience habit that contributes to my success is exercise. I came to exercise later in my life (in my forties), and now I cannot imagine not having it in my life. I either walk or do high-intensity interval training at least five days a week, and I do it from 5:00 to 6:00 a.m. during the workweek. I don't relish getting up so early, and I'm frequently very sore. But the most at peace I ever feel is when I'm finished with a hard workout or during a long walk. It's time that is just for me.

I often make connections between concepts or come up with new hypotheses during these times, when my brain is not bothered by other noise. I also think of people in my life who I want to catch up with and will send them a text during a walk just to say hello and that I'm thinking about them, or ask how they are if I know they are going through a tough time.

I nurture and develop trusting relationships by being open and vulnerable with people. I'm not a difficult person to get to know; I'm an open book about places where I struggle, and I share openly about how I'm trying to address those challenges. The older I get, the more I'm willing to be myself—to ask the difficult questions people are dancing around, to answer those difficult questions honestly when they come my way, to reach out to people even if they don't respond. I do it with kindness, but I do it regardless. People may decide they don't like me, but I'm no longer so bothered by that. Dita Von Teese had a quote in the book *Tribe of Mentors* by Timothy Ferriss that has stuck with me: "You can be the ripest, juiciest peach in the world, and there's still going to be somebody who hates peaches."

When I hear the word "resilience," the words that come to mind are: "values," "commitment," "growth," and "vulnerability."

—Deborah Nguyen, PhD
Senior Biotech Leader, Research and Development

7

Declutter your desk and computer files.

Well-being

chedule time to declutter and organize the files on your desk and computer. Decide on what system works best for you and your job responsibilities and tasks. Store the files you need and dispose of the files that you will not need to look at again.

8

Exercise.

Well-being

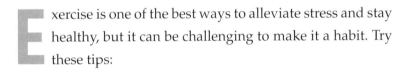xercise is one of the best ways to alleviate stress and stay healthy, but it can be challenging to make it a habit. Try these tips:

- Schedule it, just like your most important meeting.

- If you do not already have a regular exercise habit, begin small.

- If you don't like the first type of exercise you try, try a different exercise, like yoga, water aerobics, pickleball—the possibilities are almost endless. This also works if you're bored!

- Having an accountability partner can help make it a priority.

9

Express gratitude often.

Well-being, Self-awareness, Brand

F eeling and expressing gratitude with authenticity has a direct positive impact on physical and mental well-being. It generates a focus on positive emotions, strengthens social bonds, nurtures trust, and boosts resilience. Take a moment to respond to a past colleague when you see them celebrating an anniversary or posting an accomplishment, whether via a comment or a personal note. Include expressions of gratitude for your connection, for what you may have learned from them, or reflect on your work together in the past.

When giving presentations, it's not uncommon to have a list of names acknowledging contributors at the end of the talk. Make these acknowledgments more special by embedding pictures of the contributors or including their names throughout the presentation, actively incorporating references to their contributions as part of the voice-over throughout the talk instead of saving this for the acknowledgments at the end. Using storytelling to connect the content of your presentation to the contributors will make it far more authentic and ultimately make your talk more engaging for the audience.

10

Get creative with your calendar when working from home.

Well-being

With virtual meetings and hybrid work settings being the norm, it's not uncommon to end up with a day full of meetings when working from home. Sitting in back-to-back meetings in Teams, Zoom, Webex, or other platforms can take a huge toll on physical and mental well-being. If you have an hour between meetings, block it off as personal time for recharge and well-being. This is your opportunity for a midmorning workout or walking break or a midafternoon break to cook a simple but healthy dinner so you aren't reaching for unhealthy snacks or a frozen dinner at the end of the workday.

Words on resilience from Resilience Champion John Kelley

I re-energize by breaking away mentally from work or normal routines. These include exercising, proactively engaging with positive people, doing something that enables me to accomplish a meaningful task or objective (puts me in a can-do frame of mind), reading a fiction book, and reflecting on past good things that have been part of my life's journey. I do this by looking at saved personal letters, notes, emails, or cards from a wide variety of relationships. An essential resilience habit for me is good sleep.

One piece of advice out of many options to aid a person in maintaining resilience during their career is to create a positive mindset when seemingly insurmountable issues persist. A proven methodology is to tap into colleagues, family, and friends for their advice, recommendations, and out-of-the-box thinking as it pertains to issues that can test your resilience as a leader. A leader is counted on by the organization to be the person who fixes problems. Elevating your thinking in envisioning new ways to attack something the leader has not pursued can open up new approaches that can work and thereby re-energize their reservoir of resilience skills.

When I hear the word "resilience," what comes to mind are: "consistent," "even-keeled," and "calm under pressure."

—John Kelley
Chairman and Executive Director, CereHealth Corp.

11

Give intermittent fasting a try.

Well-being

ntermittent fasting is any of various meal timing schedules that cycle between voluntary fasting and non-fasting over a given period. Various benefits of intermittent fasting, independent of weight loss, have been discovered through independent research in the last few years, including reduction of inflammation, increased stress resistance, increased longevity, and a decreased incidence of diseases, including cancer and obesity. This is just one of many approaches to improve your overall well-being, but it might be worth exploring.

I started intermittent fasting after reading "Effects of Intermittent Fasting on Health, Aging, and Disease" on December 26, 2019, and lost over twenty pounds through early 2021.[1]

—Songmao (Ben) Zheng

---

1   Rafael de Cabo, PhD, and Mark P. Mattson, PhD, "Effects of Intermittent Fasting on Health, Aging, and Disease," *New England Journal of Medicine*, December 26, 2019, https://www.nejm.org/doi/full/10.1056/nejmra1905136.

12

Go to sleep.

Well-being

Getting the sleep you need is crucial to being your best at work and life. Most of us need from six to eight hours of sleep every night.

- Figure out how many hours you need to be at your best and set a schedule that works for you.

- Stay away from your computer monitor or phone at least one hour before bed. The blue spectrum of light from electronics can block the release of melatonin, which puts you to sleep.

- Practice before-bed rituals that help relax or lull you to sleep. Try a meditation sleep app, read a relaxing novel or poetry, pray, or listen to soothing music.

One of my favorite sleep meditations is from Calm, and it is called Deep Sleep Release. You can select the amount of time you would like the meditation to play, ranging from five minutes to thirty minutes in five-minute increments. It works amazingly and puts me right to sleep even when I have a monkey mind.

—Beth Kennedy

- If you wake up in the middle of the night, try the 4–7–8 breathing technique: inhale for four, hold for seven, and exhale for eight. This technique will lower your heart rate and help you get back to sleep.

13

Harness the power of meditation.

Well-being, Self-awareness

editation and mindfulness can improve work performance, personal relationships, health, and much more. Just five minutes of deep breathing, reflection, and tension release can decrease stress levels and increase overall productivity and job satisfaction. If you don't have a quiet place to meditate and clear your mind, try using your car or booking an office or single-person phone booth at work. There are numerous apps for phones and tablets that can facilitate meditation, as well as guided sessions on YouTube and other sources. Even if you don't feel you are fully harvesting the benefits of meditation, it's a worthwhile experiment.

This photo from Karthik shows a bonsai plant, which is a living gift from his leadership coach Beth Kennedy, and a Buddha statue, which was a token of appreciation from one of his cherished mentees.

14

Infuse exploration, entertainment, and fun while traveling for work.

Well-being, Connection

Traveling for work can be exhausting and stressful, especially when crossing several time zones. With a little extra planning and organization, you can make business travel an avenue for broadening your view of the world, recharging, and connecting with diverse people. Try the following:

- On the day of arrival, take a walk in the city to view the top sights or a hike in nature to experience new landscapes. Exercise is a great way to combat jet lag and enable restful overnight sleep. You'll start the next day refreshed and recharged and ready for a day of successful meetings.

- Coordinate an activity with fellow travelers from your organization or other attendees at the conference to enable teambuilding and connection.

- Give yourself an escape one evening. Maybe your favorite band is playing or there's a restaurant that looks interesting. You don't need to spend all your evenings in your hotel room!

I am grateful for the experience of working for multinational organizations in roles that required travel to East Asia and Europe for international team meetings and conferences. During several of these trips, I was able to infuse tourism through careful planning of travel, enabling me to visit many spectacular sights from the Matterhorn to the Great Wall of China and even see one of my favorite bands, Coldplay, at the iconic Wembley Stadium in London.

—Karthik Venkatakrishnan

15

Plan your vacations for the year.

Well-being, Innovation

Do you use your allotted vacation time? You probably have the best intentions to take your time off, but unless you plan it, urgency often takes over. Try to plan your trips several months in advance. Anticipating a vacation can increase well-being for weeks and even months. If traveling is not relaxing for you, try a staycation and plan fun activities, like meeting friends for a leisurely lunch or working on a house project where making progress will be exciting.

Photos from Karthik and Beth, taken in their global travels.

16

Plant something.

Well-being, Innovation

Plants can be tremendously soothing to look at and may calm you down in times of need. Plants whisper back, if you whisper to them. Don't worry about not having a "green thumb." Depending on your personal growing conditions, an easy-to-grow houseplant may be the right option to get your plant journey started, and you will be pleasantly surprised at what you can harvest!

I used to be a "plant killer," but I now have over one thousand plants, mostly orchids and tropical plants, thriving in my 450-square-foot greenhouse and home office with "innovative" setups such as semiautomatic watering! They have proven to be an essential part of my resilience journey. Find your favorite plants—an orchid grower with thirty years of experience once told me, "You will find your favorite type of orchid," and this is applicable to the broad realm of plants, such as houseplants.

—Songmao (Ben) Zheng

This collage by Songmao combines samples from his plant collection with his passion for photography.

17

Put your own oxygen mask on first.

Well-being, Self-awareness

When uncertainty or change leads to anxiety or an inability to cope, it may be tempting to first help those you care for, especially if you have a role as an advisor, manager, or team leader. However, it is critically important to first take care of yourself before you can take care of others, in order to optimally support your team with quality guidance and support. This requires you to ensure that you have the necessary fuel for physical, mental, and emotional well-being. Besides ensuring sufficient time for nutrition, sleep, and exercise to provide physical well-being, asking for help and connecting to people beyond your immediate circle of professional relationships can actively nurture mental and emotional well-being. Reciprocal empathy experienced in connection with others facing similar situations or challenges will not only diffuse the stress but also help identify constructive solutions and enable a refreshed mind so you can more effectively help others for whom you are responsible.

18

Recharge with nature.

Well-being, Innovation

I t is great to enjoy your career, but it is important to have other things that recharge your batteries. Indulge in the beauty of the outdoors—it can be as magical as watching a sunset or as simple as smelling your favorite flower. By focusing on nature, you can forget some of your work stressors, produce innovative ideas, and focus on your goals and dreams.

These photos by Songmao from his trips to US national parks speak to his love for nature and photography.

Words on resilience
from Resilience Champion
Michael J. Hanley

Spending time outside and exercising are my two preferred ways to recharge. At the start of the COVID-19 pandemic, I often found myself sitting at my desk going from virtual meeting to virtual meeting for seemingly the whole day. As a result, I started to block a fifteen-minute period each morning and afternoon to allow myself to get outside during the day for a mini recharge break.

In my area, golf courses were one of the first things to reopen after lockdown. Although I hadn't played in several years, I started picking one evening a week to golf after work. This gave me something to look forward to during even the most stressful of weeks and is a habit I have continued. My weekly golfing recharge serves as my mental reset button.

One weekly resilience habit I have is to proactively block "focus time" on my calendar on Friday afternoons, while remaining available for any business-critical meetings. I use this time to complete any outstanding deliverables from the week, which helps to give me a sense of accomplishment heading into the weekend. I also find that this makes it easier to disconnect from work over the weekend.

I would advise people who want to be more resilient to learn to accept and embrace change as it is one of the constants in life. Colleagues and projects will come and go, organizational changes will occur, professional and personal setbacks will happen, and life will throw you a curveball when you least expect it. More often than not, these events are entirely beyond our control. The only thing we can control is how we choose to react to them. I have found that taking time to reflect on these events and viewing them as potential opportunities for professional and personal growth help to build my resiliency by avoiding the natural tendency to view changes and events through the lens of negativity. Try to look for silver linings whenever and wherever you can, however faint they might be.

The words that come to mind when I think of resilience are: "bend not break," "adaptability," "toughness," and "ability to bounce back."

—Michael J. Hanley, PharmD, PhD
Scientific Director, Quantitative Clinical
Pharmacology (Oncology), Takeda Pharmaceuticals

19

Reduce commute stress and get adequate sleep with active calendar management.

Well-being

I f you work for a global organization with teams of colleagues spread across diverse time zones, it's not uncommon to have early morning meetings or late evening post-dinner meetings. It can be a challenge to balance virtual meetings and face-to-face meetings with colleagues or clients located on-site. If you have a virtual meeting that starts at 7:00 a.m. and ends at 11:00 a.m. and a face-to-face meeting in the office at 11:00 a.m., you'd have to leave home at 6:00 a.m. and take your 7:00 a.m. call from the office so you could be there for the 11:00 a.m. meeting!

Proactively block off commute time in your calendar to avoid getting into situations like this, especially if you routinely work late into the evening, leaving you without adequate sleep. This impacts your well-being, which will decrease productivity and cause burnout in the long run. It also does not make for a safe driving experience if you constantly end up driving without having slept well overnight.

20

Set aside time every day for you.

Well-being, Self-awareness

isten to your favorite music, play with your pet, meditate, or go outside for a walk. Studies show that canine affection and getting out into nature can lower your blood pressure and increase your level of dopamine. If you do not set aside time to take care of yourself, your energy gets depleted. Think of your energy as a bank account and imagine ways to make deposits daily to get the results you want and need.

21

Set yourself positive examples in your daily routine so that they become positive habits.

Well-being, Self-awareness

Being intentional about setting positive examples in your daily routine can help you live more mindfully, productively, and happily. Be specific and purposeful about the actions you need to take to establish those routines. If you cannot do exactly what you intend to do, don't feel frustrated. Focus on what you can do next on another day. Make a list of what you want to achieve in the next few days and pick the low-hanging fruits first. As you start to see the benefits of these positive daily routines, there's a much higher chance of them becoming positive habits, which can boost your resilience!

I had been struggling with keeping my apartment clean and tidy due to having too many items (e.g., plants and gadgets). I established a routine of throwing away empty shipping boxes as soon as they arrived, instead of stacking them up indefinitely. I also made an intentional effort to put things into their designated spot right away. Actions like these helped greatly in dealing with the organizational chaos.

—**Songmao (Ben) Zheng**

22

Start meetings five minutes late and end meetings five minutes early.

Well-being, Brand

Going from one meeting to the next nonstop during the workday—whether virtual or in person—is not healthy. You need time to take stretch breaks and bio-breaks, fill up your bottle of hydration or take some bites of an energy bar, make that important phone call to schedule an appointment that can only be done during work hours, gaze out of the window at some greenery to reduce eye strain, give your eyes some rest with an eye mask, or take a mini-break to browse social media posts for recharging between two intense meetings.

Give yourself and your colleagues a break by starting meetings five minutes late and ending them five minutes early. If some colleagues do arrive in the virtual room or the conference room during the five-minute interval, it's an opportunity for them to connect informally and make social conversation, the importance of which should not be underestimated.

This gorgeous park has a name

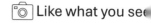

Like what you see

8:18

Sunday, August 18

Mostly Sunny
High 30°, Low 22°

Photo of the Ngorongoro Conservation Area by Melissa Corcoran.

23

Start your day with a minute of virtual exploration.

Well-being

D on't ignore the picture that shows up on your Windows spotlight startup screen when you switch on your PC. Rather than logging in and immediately answering emails or joining your first meeting of the day, take fifteen seconds to let your brain absorb and react to the picture you see and give feedback on whether you like it. Even better, if it's something you really like, take another thirty seconds to jot down the name of the location in a journal of places you may want to visit someday or art and architecture you want to see. The more you engage and tell the computer whether you liked what you saw, the more likely you are to see images you like in the coming weeks, months, and years. It's a great way to start your day in a positive frame of mind before you begin working.

24

Stay hydrated with your drink of choice.

Well-being

S everal recent large-scale studies have demonstrated the health benefits of coffee consumption and demystified some suspected and hypothetical harmful effects.[2] A combination regimen of coffee and tea can do wonders for balancing energy and nutrition benefits. For those who don't get along well with strongly caffeinated drinks, simply staying hydrated with water or trying diluted coffee or tea could be a path forward to gain much-needed energy.

---

2   Luigi Barrea et al., "Coffee Consumption, Health Benefits and Side Effects: A Narrative Review and Update for Dietitians and Nutritionists," *Critical Reviews in Food Science and Nutrition* 63, no. 9 (2023): 1238–1261, https://doi.org/10.1080/10408398.2021.1963207.

Beth begins her day with a mindful cup of coffee with warm unsweetened vanilla almond milk or Earl Grey tea in her favorite fish mug.

Karthik often starts his day with a cup of coffee with milk and sweetener or a cup of sweetened tea brewed with milk and aromatics like cardamom and freshly grated ginger.

A morning regimen for Songmao is unsweetened coffee, preferably cold-brewed, followed by unsweetened green tea.

25

Stress can be your friend.

Well-being, Self-awareness

Stress is your response to daily demands. There are two types of stress: "eustress," which is good stress, and "distress," which is negative stress. *Eustress* can include having the right amount of challenge in your career and using your strengths to put you in "flow," where you are energized and lose track of time. *Distress* is the negative stress that puts you in burnout mode. For some, distress is being in a career role that does not use their strengths or working in an organization in which the internal politics become toxic and get in the way of productivity. Every person is wired differently and what may stress out one person may motivate another. Be aware of your own stress triggers, name them, and then let them go.

26

Switch your
work environment.

Well-being, Innovation

I f some of your work (for example, reading and reflecting) can be done beyond the confines of your usual work-space, for an occasional change of pace and recharge, find a spot without distractions (e.g., common workspace in your office, coffee shop, or library) in which to work. Done in a different ambience, this can take the boredom out of mundane tasks that require you to stare at a computer or read through papers, where the reward following completion of the activity can be a stroll in the park or your favorite treat at the coffee shop bakery. Maybe it can even be timed to coincide with meeting a friend who is scheduled to show up when you finish working, serving as a stimulus to timebox and complete the work.

Words on resilience from Resilience Champion Lisa J. Benincosa

Photo courtesy of Roche Pharmaceuticals

A resilience habit that's important to me is to take time for myself. Quiet reflection takes my mind off the present tasks and pressures.

It is important for me to strike a work-life balance. To reduce stress, I make time for important family priorities. It is stressful to feel guilty about missing either family or work events. With scheduling, a good balance can be achieved so at least the most important events are balanced.

My brand is "pragmatic." I see the big picture and therefore can prioritize and focus on what is important. This can be helpful for others while giving me professional satisfaction.

The words that come to mind when I think of resilience are: "strength," "balance," and "health."

—Lisa J. Benincosa, PhD
Senior Vice President
Clinical Pharmacology Strategy Division, Allucent

27

Take mini-breaks between meetings and projects.

Well-being

"Sitting is the new smoking." One study found that of 794,577 participants, people who sit the most, compared to people who sit the least, have a greater risk of disease and death: 112 percent increased risk of diabetes, 147 percent increased risk of cardiovascular events like heart attack and stroke, and 90 percent increased risk of death from cardiovascular events.[3] Prolonged sitting without getting up to move around can also potentially lead to deep vein thrombosis, the formation of a blood clot in a vein deep in the body. Research has also shown that people who take five-minute breaks every hour tend to be more productive than those who work straight through. Set a timer or automatic reminder on your phone, smartwatch, or calendar to get up and move. Do some stretches throughout the day to ease tension in the back, neck, arms, and legs. It's a little investment in your well-being that can go a long way.

3   E. G. Wilmot et al., "Sedentary Time in Adults and the Association with Diabetes, Cardiovascular Disease and Death: Systematic Review and Meta-Analysis. *Diabetologia* 55, no. 11 (November 2012): 2895–2905, https://doi.org/10.1007/s00125-012-2677-z.

28

Use a to-do list.

Well-being, Self-awareness

Keep a comprehensive to-do list for the week and check off items as they are completed. If tasks that were not on the to-do list come up and get done during the day, take a moment to add them to the to-do list and check them off. Seeing a to-do list with completed items provides valuable positive reinforcement that will fuel you to complete the remaining items and provide a feeling of satisfaction. Even if there are items that remain and carry over onto next week's list, the positive reinforcement that comes from seeing the checked-off items can be valuable.

To-Do List

- ☑ Prepare a presentation for investor meeting
- ☐ Finish writing research paper
- ☑ Register for webinar
- ☑ Connect with past colleague

29

Vegetables and fruits can boost your energy.

Well-being

I f you are too "lazy" or too busy to peel off the skin of a fruit, easy-to-handle, ready-to-consume fruits and vegetables, like bananas, citrus fruits, organic baby carrots, cherry tomatoes, goji berries, blueberries, and blackberries are your best friends. Eating carbohydrate-rich fruits replenishes your glycogen levels and keeps you energized. Additionally, fruits contain simple carbohydrates that your body easily breaks down into glucose to give you a quick boost of energy. Many vegetables and fruits contain phytonutrients like flavonoids that have beneficial anti-inflammatory effects and can protect your cells from oxidative damage that can lead to disease.

Songmao took this photo during his visit to a market-place in Seattle.

30

Write in a personal journal.

Well-being, Self-awareness

Take time even just once a week to write in a personal journal. It is amazing how writing things down can help you focus on what matters most, reduce stress, and be a recharge. It can give you a chance to put things in perspective and help you solve problems and be less reactive. Keeping a journal to track your travel adventures will remind you of why it is so important to plan vacations and take a break from work. You can either write by hand or electronically.

If you are concerned that there is no way you will find time to write in a journal with all the other personal and professional demands in life, try setting a timer for five minutes; you will be amazed at how much you will be able to write.

I use a journal that has prompts in it, and I find it keeps me focused and does not take up a lot of time.

—Beth Kennedy

31

Accept and encourage feedback from others.

Self-awareness, Brand

A sk your friends, clients, and colleagues for constructive feedback. You will not know where to improve unless you know what isn't working. Ask individuals whom you trust and who know you well. Decide on which feedback can add impact to your career and begin by focusing on one small step.

32

Be curious and open to your feelings.

Self-awareness, Well-being

"Have the courage that your heart is
big enough to be able to take in a whole
rainbow of different feelings and emotions."

This quote by Rev. Paul Tesshin Silverman, Zen Buddhist priest, illustrates the importance of allowing yourself to be more accepting and present to a roller coaster of emotions.[4] Be curious and ask questions, rather than leaping immediately to problem-solving or avoidance, when life takes you through unplanned twists and turns.

---

4   Paul Tesshin Silverman quoted in Sherrie Dulworth, "Why Was It So Hard to Bear Witness to My Father's Final Days?" *Boston Globe*, last updated June 4, 2023, https://www.bostonglobe.com/2023/06/04/opinion/bearing-witness-when-a-loved-one-is-dying/.

Words on resilience from Resilience Champion Neeraj Gupta

Photo courtesy of Takeda Pharmaceuticals

One piece of advice for cultivating resilience in both career and life is to embrace adaptability. Life is unpredictable, and being able to adapt to changing circumstances is key to resilience. This involves a mindset shift that welcomes change as an opportunity for growth rather than a threat. Fostering a flexible mindset allows individuals to approach challenges with openness and creativity. Instead of resisting change, being adaptable means exploring new ways of thinking and problem-solving. This flexibility enables individuals to pivot when faced with unexpected obstacles, finding alternative routes toward their goals.

Developing a diverse skill set contributes to resilience. The more skills and knowledge one possesses, the better equipped one is to navigate different situations. Continuous learning and upskilling not only broaden one's capabilities but also provide a sense of confidence when confronting unfamiliar territory.

Surrounding oneself with mentors, colleagues, friends, or a community that provides encouragement and guidance fosters resilience. These connections offer different perspectives and insights and serve as a source of motivation during challenging times.

Taking care of one's physical and mental well-being ensures the stamina needed to persevere through tough situations. Cultivating a positive attitude and practicing gratitude can help reframe setbacks as opportunities for learning and growth.

In essence, embracing adaptability as a core principle, constantly learning and diversifying skills, fostering a support network, and prioritizing self-care are key strategies for building resilience in both career and life. The ability to adapt, learn, and maintain a positive perspective empowers individuals to navigate uncertainties and setbacks, emerging stronger and more resilient in the face of adversity.

A habit of mine that significantly contributes to both my success and personal fulfillment is practicing mindfulness. Every day, I allocate a few minutes for mindfulness. This routine serves as an anchor, grounding me for the day ahead. It allows me to cultivate self-awareness, which is crucial for resilience. Mindfulness helps me manage stress effectively. In the face of challenges, I've learned to acknowledge my emotions, understand their root causes, and respond rather than react impulsively. This approach has been transformative, enabling me to navigate difficult situations with greater clarity and composure. Furthermore, mindfulness fosters a sense of gratitude and perspective. It encourages me to appreciate small moments, fostering a positive outlook even amidst chaos. This outlook helps me bounce back from setbacks, finding lessons and opportunities within adversity.

It is important to do this consistently. By engaging in this practice daily, it has become a natural part of my routine, reinforcing its impact on my resilience. It's a habit that doesn't demand significant time but yields immense benefits. Most times, I don't need to plan for it now.

Through mindfulness, I've cultivated resilience not just in my professional endeavors but also in personal relationships and overall well-being. It's a foundational practice that aligns with my values, promoting a balanced and fulfilling life. This daily commitment to mindfulness has become a pillar supporting my growth, enabling me to face challenges with a sense of calm and adaptability, ultimately contributing to both my success and personal fulfillment.

Focusing on resilience has been pivotal in shaping my career success. It's been a guiding principle that transformed how I approach challenges, setbacks, and opportunities. In my career, resilience has been the cornerstone of my growth. Instead of seeing obstacles as roadblocks, I've learned to view them as stepping stones. Each setback became an opportunity for learning and growth. This mindset has enabled me to persist through difficulties and fostered perseverance and adaptability.

Resilience has also empowered me to take calculated risks. I've been more willing to embrace change, knowing that setbacks are part of the journey. This openness to new experiences has led me to discover unexplored opportunities and expand my skill set, ultimately contributing to my professional success. Moreover, resilience has shaped how I interact with others in the workplace. It has helped me navigate conflicts, setbacks, and stressful situations with a calm and composed demeanor. This ability to maintain composure and offer support during challenging times has earned me trust and respect among colleagues and superiors, fostering healthy work relationships and collaborations.

Beyond career success, focusing on resilience has enriched my personal life profoundly. It has deepened my relationships by allowing me to approach conflicts with empathy and understanding. It has helped me appreciate the importance of self-care, setting boundaries, and recognizing when to seek help or support.

Overall, resilience has provided me with the mental fortitude to withstand adversities, the flexibility to adapt to changing circumstances, and the courage to pursue my aspirations. It has been the driving force behind my career achievements and a more fulfilling and balanced life, allowing me to thrive professionally and personally, no matter the challenges I encounter along the way.

When I hear the word "resilience," the words that come to mind are: "adaptability," "perseverance," and "determination."

—Neeraj Gupta, PhD, FCP
Executive Director and Head of Quantitative
Clinical Pharmacology (Oncology)
Takeda Pharmaceuticals

33

Begin your day with morning intentions.

Self-awareness, Well-being

Positive affirmations can unleash your creativity, open your mind, and energize you for the day. Some people do this when they first wake up; others find it's easier to do with their first cup of coffee or before an important meeting. Think about what you would like your day to look like and how you want to feel. Examples include "calm and confident," "patient and focused," or "energized and strategic."

34

Create a dream board or vision journal.

Self-awareness, Innovation, Brand

What do you want your personal and professional future to look like? It's easy to get caught up in day-to-day demands, but before you know it, another year has gone by and your life is not what you want it to be. Get a notebook or journal and use it to dream without limits. Begin by focusing on small goals you would like to accomplish in six months, one year, three years, and five years. You can be specific and add categories like career, personal, well-being, financial, travel, connection, and innovation. Every time you accomplish a dream or vision, record the date. In time, you will look back on dreams you thought were impossible to achieve when you wrote them down and be amazed at the ease with which they were accomplished. This will not only advance your career but your personal life as well.

My own personal example was when I wrote my first book. It was a dream I had for many years, but it became a reality when I wrote it down as a five-year goal. *Career ReCharge: Five Strategies to Boost Resilience and Beat Burnout* was published within the next three years.

—Beth Kennedy

Beth's dream board that led to her first book.

35

Create your own good luck.

Self-awareness, Well-being

"Behind bad luck comes good luck."

—Lao Tzu

We all experience bad luck or unexpected situations. How we deal with them affects our well-being. The ancient phrase above is here to help: It means that sometimes a bad situation can lead to a good outcome or that good things can happen after bad things. It is similar to other expressions like "every cloud has a silver lining." It is a way of being optimistic and hopeful when facing difficulties or challenges, whether at work or in life. Try to encourage someone who is going through a hard time using this method and share your own experiences. After all, we are often creators of our own luck. Drawing strengths from hardships and bad luck, as well as learning from past experiences, may be just what we need to have more good luck!

36

Cultivate a beginner's mindset.

Self-awareness, Innovation

"In the beginner's mind there are many possibilities,
but in the expert's, there are few."

—Shunryu Suzuki, Zen Mind, Beginner's Mind

As this quote describes, when you have a beginner's mind, it means you approach the world through a mindset of possibilities. The term "beginner's mindset" is translated from *shoshin*, which comes from Zen Buddhism and means looking at every situation you're placed in as if it's the first time you are seeing it. A beginner does not have any expectations or past experiences to limit their view of a situation and has a curiosity toward something new. This often leads to innovative ideas.

Try developing this mindset even when you already know something or have lots of experience with a topic. Although an expert may know a lot, an expert mindset can be a narrow point of view that can block you from finding new and better ways to solve a problem. Notice how you are showing up to innovative ideas being presented at meetings or to change overall. How can you introduce a beginner's mindset into your day?

37

Cultivate equanimity.

Self-awareness

eff Warren, a meditation teacher on the Calm app, defines equanimity as "the capacity to let your experience be what it is, without trying to fight it and negotiate with it. It's like an inner smoothness."[5] When we practice equanimity in the face of stressors, it is easier to accept and move forward, without going down the burnout escalator.

> I find that whenever I am dealing with a very stressful situation, just saying the word "equanimity" calms my nervous system and lets me react in a calm and proactive manner.
>
> **—Beth Kennedy**

---

5   Dan Harris, Jeff Warren, and Carlyle Adler, *Meditation for Fidgety Skeptics* (New York: Harmony, 2017), 45.

38

Embrace change and transition.

Self-awareness

A dapt to new situations and opportunities with a positive and flexible attitude. Change is inevitable and often beneficial, but it can also be challenging and stressful. Facing change becomes easier when you think in terms of growth and learning instead of seeing your identity as a rigid, unchangeable set of traits and skills. A growth mindset allows you to see change as an opportunity to develop new abilities, expand your horizons, and discover fresh possibilities.

Your own perception is an important part of a change. The next time there's a change at work, such as a change in management or a new office space or schedule, see it as a transition and a chance to learn and grow rather than as a crisis.

A great strategy to implement during a transition is called the stress equation, first termed by the psychologist Albert

Ellis.[6] The stress equation is A + B = C, in which A represents the stressful event or specific change, B represents your beliefs about that event, and C represents what you feel and how you react afterward—the consequence.

- For example, you just found out that next month, you need to be physically back in the office two days a week. This would be the A in the equation.

- Your feelings may be frustration from the time spent commuting and annoyance because you are more productive working from home (B).

- The option of possibly job hunting would be the C.

An alternative response could be the following:

- The organization is concerned about engagement and is trying to get us back to the office but only two days a week (A).

- I enjoy being full-time at home, but maybe I will be more energized being back in the office and seeing my colleagues in person (B).

- Although this is not what I wanted, I will give it a try and then decide whether I will stay or leave, since I presently have a great career fit (C).

---

6   "The ABC Model of Stress Reduction" can be accessed at https://www. dartmouth.edu/eap/Review%20ABC%20Model%20of%20Stress.doc#:~:text =Dr%20Albert%20Ellis%2C%20founder%20of,A%2BB%3DC%20equation.

Words on resilience from Resilience Champion Melissa Corcoran

Focusing on my resilience has helped me weather life changes. One of those changes was when I was hit by a car while walking to the train station several years ago. I wound up with several injuries, the most significant of which was a severe concussion. The aftereffects of the concussion took months to subside, but most of my other injuries healed relatively quickly. All in all, I was the luckiest person on the face of the earth that night.

When I look back on all that's transpired since, I realize that resilience helped me remake my life—everything from creating a different lifestyle to being willing to take more risks ("I got hit by a car, I think I can deal with relocating").

I recharge myself with beauty, entering other worlds through books and movies, and laughter. Beauty feeds my soul, and I am fortunate to live in a place where I am surrounded by it. I have always loved to read and watch movies; one of the ties between me and my dad was playing "my ten favorite movies." It's from my dad that I get my sense of humor, which is a way to release stress. Laughing with other people is a way I connect with them.

A daily habit of mine is gratitude. I try every day to articulate at least one thing for which I am grateful. Sometimes it's as basic as a roof over my head and food on my table. I've even been known to express gratitude to my printer for working properly when I need it to!

To be more resilient, I suggest being aware of the kinds of stories you tell yourself. Emily Esfahani Smith, in her book *The Power of Meaning: Crafting a Life That Matters*, talks about the research into our personal narratives and how those narratives impact our lives. Narratives can be redemptive, show us that we have more control in our lives than we think we do, and add meaning to our lives.

I also suggest hiring the experts. Whether it's a career coach, financial planner, or therapist, their expertise can make your life better and allow you to devote your time and energy to using your skills and talents.

When I hear the word "resilience," I think: "bounce," "flexibility," "change," and "risk."

—Melissa Corcoran
Project Manager

39

Incorporate scenario planning and decision trees.

Self-awareness

Scenario planning is a structured process for making key strategic decisions in the face of an uncertain future. It involves sketching out three or four external scenarios and then identifying the internal actions to take to prepare for, and respond to, one or more of those scenarios. Scenario planning can help you anticipate risks and opportunities, test your assumptions, and adapt to changing conditions.

Prioritize your scenarios based on their likelihood and impact (e.g., using the RISK SCORE = likelihood x impact), and build that into your decision tree so you can make real-time adjustments to your activities so as to optimize the outcome.

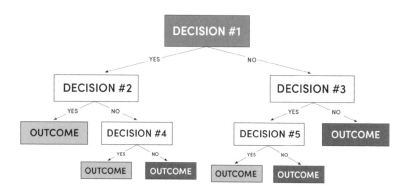

40

Invest your time in what's most important.

Self-awareness

Time management is a challenge every day. Some techniques, however, have stood the test of time. One of these is the Eisenhower Matrix, or the Urgent/Important Matrix.

Dwight D. Eisenhower, the thirty-fourth president of the United States, credited his high productivity to a simple quadrant system he created for organizing the tasks he needed to get done. First, he categorized each task as "urgent" or "not urgent." Next, he decided if each task was "important" or "not important." Each task then fell into one of the four quadrants of his matrix.

When you organize your tasks into these four categories, you can decide what to do now, what to schedule, what to delegate, and what to eliminate.

continued

	URGENT	NOT URGENT
IMPORTANT	Quadrant I *urgent and* *important* **STRESS**	Quadrant II *not urgent* *but important* **RESILIENCE**
NOT IMPORTANT	Quadrant III *urgent but* *not important* **DELEGATE**	Quadrant IV *not urgent and* *not important* **ELIMINATE**

Be deliberate about scheduling Quadrant 2 activities (not urgent but important). This is where planning for and investing time in your future takes place. Keep a journal tracking Quadrant 2 activities (e.g., continuous learning, mentoring, financial planning) on a weekly basis for positive reinforcement, and you will notice that urgency is no longer controlling your career and life. As an example, the authors consider writing this book over the past year as a memorable Quadrant 2 activity.

41

Learn to cope with ambiguity while proactively seeking clarity.

Self-awareness

One trait of being resilient is the ability to handle ambiguity effectively. We like to have direction, instructions, and situations that are clear-cut, but sometimes the complexity of work (and life) makes that impossible. Some examples of ambiguity at work include waiting for an important update to complete a project, working toward an unclear or evolving goal, working in an undefined role, or planning around a big change. Coping with ambiguity can be quite challenging, but it can also help you develop your coping skills, creativity, and resilience. When faced with unresolvable ambiguity, here are a few tips:

- Use your best judgment, rely on your experiences and intuition, and be open to feedback and correction when making decisions without having all needed information.

- Ask clarifying questions, seek different perspectives, challenge your and your team's assumptions, and test your solutions in virtual settings (e.g., through simulations, projections, and scenario planning) to solve problems innovatively.

- Communicate your goals, expectations, progress, and challenges with your stakeholders and team members.

Realizing that ambiguity is an unavoidable part of work and life in general and chaos is part of the norm is one step forward in coping with ambiguity successfully.

42

Let go of
negative stressors.

Self-awareness, Well-being

When you feel an emotion caused by a negative event or a toxic person, take a few deep breaths and let it go. There are some situations that you do not have any control over, so don't waste your energy on them.

I like to imagine putting the emotion or frustrating person into a beautiful hot-air balloon and letting it float way above the clouds so I can no longer see it and it no longer wastes my energy.

—Beth Kennedy

43

Listen to your gut.

Self-awareness

Sometimes, even if you've gathered all the data and a decision seems obvious based on an algorithm, a scientific method, or a quantitative analysis, if your gut instinct tells you that the decision may not be right, sleep on it before making the decision. Often coming back to the problem with a fresh, rested mind or soliciting an additional neutral opinion can bring clarity to the problem at hand and enable the right decision.

Words on resilience from Resilience Champion Edna F. Choo

Photo courtesy of Genentech

I recharge by "switching off" with exercise, travel, and being outdoors in the fresh air—I find these keep me sane. I am good to myself by indulging in a day off or getting a massage.

My resilience habits include:

- Not letting the little things bother me and picking my battles

- Being able to look in the mirror and know that I am my authentic self

- Knowing my colleagues as people, rejoicing with them in their professional and personal triumphs and milestones (promotions, weddings, births), and showing empathy during tough times; this is the greatest fulfillment in my professional life

continued

To be more resilient, I advise people to:

- Not sweat the small stuff

- Be humble; be at peace with knowing that you are not indispensable

- Be calm and lean on others during a "storm"

- Know that work is always going to be there, and you are allowed to take a break

When I hear the word "resilience," what comes to mind is: "strong," "brave/gutsy," and "resourceful."

—Edna F. Choo, PhD
Senior Director and Distinguished Scientist
Drug Metabolism and Pharmacokinetics, Genentech

44

Live and let live.

Self-awareness, Brand

Try not to use the same benchmark for others as for yourself. Nobody is perfect. Understanding and appreciating your own limitations, as well as others', can reduce stress and mitigate frustrations.

45

Manage your "yes" reflex.

Self-awareness, Brand

Sometimes, saying no is saying yes to what matters most in your life. The next time someone asks you to add another responsibility to your overloaded plate, don't answer right away. Tell the person you will get back to them. Take time to evaluate the situation and determine whether it will add or take away from your priorities and whether it would energize you or deplete your energy. Then, and only then, give the person an answer you can live with. It is better to say no to a project than not be able to fulfill it to your satisfaction. The point is not to ignore commitments but to make sure you don't overwhelm yourself.

When I realize that my current commitments and capacity do not permit me to accept an invitation to collaborate or contribute to an exciting and important new initiative or working group, rather than feeling disappointed, I often see it as an opportunity to recommend a current or past mentee or colleague who may be earlier in their career and qualified to take the same opportunity, so it becomes a win-win for everyone. The joy of finding opportunities for others to help them succeed effectively counters the initial disappointment felt in saying no to a potentially exciting opportunity.

—Karthik Venkatakrishnan

46

Move out of your bias blind spot.

Self-awareness

The "bias blind spot" is a cognitive bias that can cause you to be less aware of your own biases than those of others and to assume that they're more susceptible to biases than you are. For example, the bias blind spot can cause you to assume that another person's stance is influenced by various biases, whereas your own stance is perfectly rational and well-justified. Because the bias blind spot can strongly influence you in a variety of domains and circumstances, it's important to recognize it and mitigate its effect on yourself. Be grateful if your colleagues share their honest feedback with you, even if that means acknowledging and apologizing for unconscious behaviors or unintended outcomes. Ask for clarity in a genuine, curious manner as that will help build trust and more effective and harmonious working relationships.

47

Name your emotions.

Self-awareness, Well-being

An important strategy for building emotional resilience is to name your emotions. It has been shown to decrease activity in the part of the brain responsible for reacting emotionally and to channel it to the part of the brain responsible for more analytical thinking. Whether in a work or personal situation, this can be an effective step for managing your feelings and avoiding being overly reactive with others.

Here are four steps you can take to name your feelings:

1. Identify the emotion. Begin by taking a moment to identify what you're feeling. Is it frustration, exhaustion, joy, or something else?

2. Name the emotion. Once you've identified the emotion, give it a name. For example, if you're feeling exhausted, you might say, "I'm not quite myself today as I am exhausted."

3. Acknowledge the emotion. Acknowledge that the emotion is there and that it's okay to feel that way. Don't try to ignore the emotion. Emotions are a healthy part of life.

4. Express the emotion. Find a healthy way to express the emotion even if it's not right away—you may need to wait till the timing is right or talk with a trusted colleague. Other ways to express emotions include talking to a close friend or a therapist, writing in a journal, or doing something creative like painting or drawing.

48

Normalize failure.

Self-awareness, Well-being

E veryone likes to win and be successful, but failure is a part of life. Normalize failure as a mindset to help you embrace more challenges, take greater risks, seek constructive feedback, and improve your performance and likelihood of success. One strategy is to define success by setting realistic and meaningful goals for yourself and your team. Establish an environment that acknowledges that people can improve in the future, learn from the circumstances, and be accountable for their actions to set you and your team up for success in the future.

Words on resilience from Resilience Champion Erik Modahl

My story of resiliency started when I was little and continues to this day. Personal and professional storylines are blurred. I left Washington state in 1982 because I did not have a clear "why" I should teach music and live in the Pacific Northwest.

After a year of traveling around the US and Canada, my "why" was challenged again with careers in music, the hotel industry, and eventually working for a coffee distribution company.

I struck out on my own venture in November 2015. Beantrust began as a business-to-business distribution and event business. It became a great success and on March 3, 2020, I purchased a small corner store with the purpose of creating a local coffee bar.

And then, when the pandemic happened, I was able to pivot from the distribution business to an online business and personally deliver coffee to people's homes for six months. I also shipped coffee around the world and facilitated Zoom events. I had lots of help and the trust of the community.

In October 2020, beantrust coffee bar opened up for business in the Cove Village in Beverly, Massachusetts. We have experienced a successful and fulfilling business. The distribution and event business has also come back to be highly profitable and extremely satisfying.

I feel strongly aligned with the beantrust brand of excellence, integrity, and creativity in bringing old-world hospitality alive in our present fast-paced, data-driven world. My personal and career goal of creating genuine connections gives me insight into furthering my mission of cultivating community.

My days begin in quietness: rest, thinking, breath work, coffee, writing thoughts in my journal, and often going for a walk in the woods. This gives me the needed momentum to go into my day, connecting with friends, problem-solving, doing tasks, persevering, gaining perspective, finding resonance, all of which gives me joy, creativity, and flow. My hope is to close my day with quietness, thoughts of gratitude, and sleeping well.

My biggest and most profound example of resiliency is found within my relationship with Diane, my wife of thirty-five years. Diane has trusted and believed in me. She is a great help. She encourages me to grow, experiment, and dream.

Focusing on resilience has contributed to my professional and personal success. Remaining in the status quo and just getting by is not what I want, but oftentimes I have settled for that because change is such a hard thing for me.

As I look back on my life and as I look forward, I welcome the opportunities of coming out of hard places. To come to a better place after I've been brought down gives me great fulfillment in believing and trusting in my mission. Perseverance, not giving up, regrouping and finding my essence, reflecting, and going forth with the energy of Mount Vesuvius of who I am! I would have it no other way. Deeply thankful.

My resilience words are: "why," "help," and "trust."

—Erik Modahl
Founder of beantrust coffee bar, Coffee Curator,
and Neighborhood Community Builder

49

Observe the observable, control the controllable, and accept the uncertainty of life.

Self-awareness, Well-being

Try to enjoy life as it happens and not worry too much about what might or might not happen next. Life is unpredictable and full of surprises, but you can miss out on the present moment if you're too focused on anticipating and planning for the future. Having said that, you can still focus on what you can see, observe, and influence and not waste your energy dwelling on what you can't control. This mindset will help you cope with uncertainty and stress and let you extract the best from your circumstances.

50

Own your mistakes, embrace them, learn from them, and move on.

Self-awareness, Brand

We are all human and human beings make mistakes. If you have developed the habit of criticizing and berating yourself for everything that goes wrong in your life, you may have a hard time moving past it. You may even have lost some of your self-confidence and inspiration for life. On the other hand, if you habitually try to shift the blame to something or someone else, it can result in tension in the workplace and in your life. A useful strategy is to objectively assess whether you have responsibility toward an undesirable outcome, regardless of with whom you are working or living. Being brutally honest with yourself can oftentimes make you realize that it isn't that difficult to admit mistakes. Learn from them and let that push you out of the chaos in order to move on.

51

Recognize that all feelings are messengers.

Self-awareness, Well-being

Treat all feelings as your friends: They are messengers carrying important information to direct your attention and focus. The key is learning to pay attention to them and the underlying messages.

Ignoring how your body feels can be disastrous in the long run. For example, when you feel tired, your body tells you to rest, slow down, pause for a minute, or simply let go. Watch for signs of stress; an unfortunate side effect of stress is a diminished awareness of how we feel. Notably, headaches and stomach issues can disguise stress, which requires you to find their root causes when physical symptoms occur.

It's easy to slip into burnout because we don't notice and manage our feelings and physical conditions as quickly and effectively as possible. To combat this, start by identifying whether there is any linkage between your stressful feelings and physical discomfort and then figure out what triggers those feelings or symptoms. The correct diagnosis is a crucial step toward problem-solving, so embrace your feelings, including those that are seemingly negative.

52

Reflect on your *ikigai* to maximize professional fulfillment.

Self-awareness, Brand

*I*kigai is a Japanese concept that means your "reason for being." It is the intersection of what you are good at, what you love to do, what the world needs, and what you can be paid for.

Ideally, professional success and personal fulfillment are maximized if your job accountabilities are at that perfect intersection. Of course, this is not always the case, but the more you can seek and nurture this alignment, the greater your fulfillment will be in life and work.

Being aware of your ikigai is the first step and will help you discover your personal and professional brand.

- Think about your favorite job and write down three reasons why it was so satisfying.

- Write down one or two of your career accomplishments that you're particularly proud of.

continued

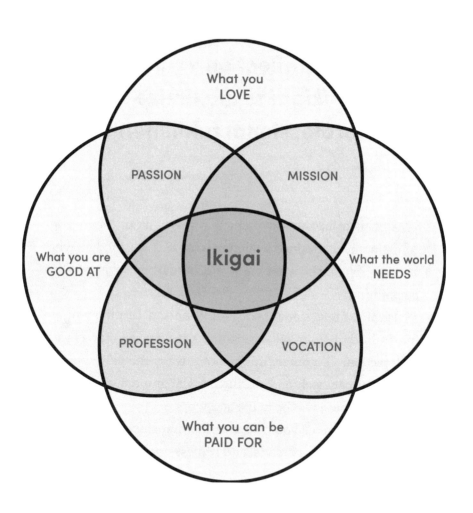

- Identify and write down your strengths, going beyond your skills.

- See if you can differentiate which of your strengths truly energize you. When you use your strengths, you are passionate and your productivity is maximized.

Use this self-awareness of your ikigai to steer development conversations with your manager or mentor, thereby helping identification of strength-aligned opportunities to enhance your productivity and value and let you shine.

If you have a role as a people manager or mentor, the concept of ikigai is equally valuable in helping steer conversations with direct reports or mentees to encourage the process of discovering their ikigai and brand, thereby promoting trust and maximizing their performance and happiness.

I have regularly used the ikigai framework in development conversations with my direct reports and mentees and also as a framework in approaching conversations with my mentors and managers regarding my own career trajectory. It helps define the right stretch goals, special assignments, and opportunities for continuous learning and upskilling aligned with one's aspirations and strengths, thereby maximizing engagement, productivity, and impact, directly enabling professional success and personal fulfilment.

—**Karthik Venkatakrishnan**

53

Reframe negative thoughts for positive action.

Self-awareness, Well-being

Rumination is a mental process of thinking about something over and over and attaching negative emotions to it. It often creates stress and needs to be managed to prevent negativity from taking over.

Use a traffic light strategy to prevent rumination:

- When you feel a negative thought, the first step is RED: Stop, pause, and breathe.

Photo by Songmao (Ben) Zheng.

- Then move to YELLOW: Reframe the situation and turn the negative thoughts into motivation for improvement or change. For example, reframe "I'm so stressed out" to "I need to set better boundaries this week and recharge."

- At GREEN, articulate a specific strategy: "I will turn off my computer at 6:00 p.m. and focus on making a healthy dinner."

54

See the glass as half-full.

Self-awareness, Brand

See problems as opportunities. Be a cautious optimist rather than a pessimist. This will inspire commitment and channel positive energy from those around you. There are always reasons why something won't succeed or why an idea may be too risky, unprecedented, or unusual to support. Often, these are situations of high risk but high reward if successful. Approaching such situations with cautious optimism rather than pessimism will motivate everyone to bring their best to address the challenge. Putting your best foot forward with confidence will maximize the likelihood of success, while a mindset that is apprehensive will translate to a lack of confidence and inability to perform at your best, thereby decreasing the chances of success.

Words on resilience from Resilience Champion Chen Chen

I recognize that I possess a distinct professional brand. This brand garners trust among new professional contacts yet simultaneously sets high expectations. My approach is to overlook these expectations, maintain focus, and dedicate myself to quality work.

Part of my resilience is that I'm selective about forging relationships, understanding that not all connections will flourish. When a relationship doesn't work out, I take it as a learning opportunity and a chance to better understand myself. Over the years, this process has helped me discover my true self and define the kind of trustworthy relationships I seek.

I've also learned the importance of self-care. Each challenge is a learning curve, teaching me to distinguish between what truly merits resilience and what does not.

When I contemplate resilience, certain words resonate with me: "uncertainty," "ultimatum," "purpose," and "internal peace."

—Chen Chen
Tech Executive, Silicon Valley startups

55

Talk to yourself in creative, positive, and constructive ways.

Self-awareness, Well-being, Innovation

Almost everyone talks to themselves, consciously or unconsciously. It can be a healthy and productive habit, as long as you do it in a positive and constructive way. Use self-talk as an opportunity to integrate information you have collected when faced with a problem or when you need to make a decision. When you find negative thoughts are clouding your judgment, use positive and compassionate affirmations to turn your "mind boat" around. Sometimes, it helps to use second- or third-person pronouns when talking to yourself. This can take off some pressure and allow you to evaluate the situation and rethink your decisions from a distance.

A useful technique is to think out loud instead of only in your head. The behavior of talking may further trigger solution-finding. If you find it difficult to organize your thoughts, use a pen and a piece of paper to write down the critical information before "making a speech" to yourself. The self-talk does not need to be motivational but should be fit-for-purpose.

56

Understand and focus attention on your circle of control.

Self-awareness

An understanding of one's circle of control is a critical component of time and energy management. Focus energy on the core of the circle that represents what is within your direct control. Pay attention to things that are in the middle ring, which include what is within the sphere of influence, if not within one's direct control. Do not spend time worrying about things that are in the outer ring, because, despite being potentially worrisome, you have no control or influence on those matters. Choose your battles and identify the areas of positive influence. Adapting focus to the inner circles and eliminating the distracting thoughts and anxiety that stem from the outer circle will eventually allow the inner and middle circles to grow in size relative to the outer circle, expanding influence and impact in your professional life, mitigating anxiety, and bringing personal fulfillment.

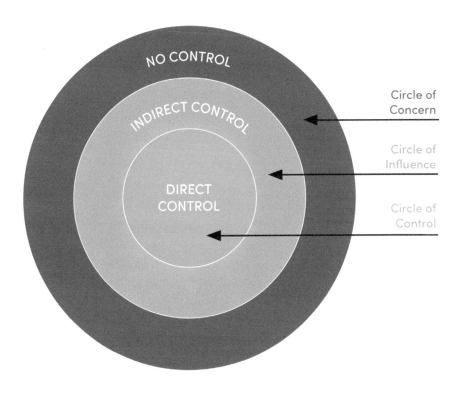

57

Unleash the child within you!

Self-awareness, Well-being, Innovation

Living up to the many written and unwritten social norms and expectations associated with adulthood can weigh us down sometimes. When the going gets tough in life, unleashing your inner child and rejoicing in doing so can create a positive and optimistic approach to life and work. Give yourself permission to keep the childhood spark alive in you, seek out the simple pleasures in life, and experience what it's like to be a kid again. Whether you blow bubbles at the beach, watch a kiddie cartoon on TV, eat a bowl of multicolored, flavored cereal for breakfast, ride a swing in the neighborhood park, or bounce on the trampoline in your backyard, break free from any sense of shame or restraint that prohibits you from letting your inner child out and enjoying such activities once in a while. It can be immensely valuable for recharge and well-being.

58

Be a solution provider.

Brand

Focus on providing solutions. Look for ways to overcome problems rather than dwelling on the past or the negative aspects (e.g., failures). You can do this by identifying the root cause of the issues you face(d), brainstorming possible alternatives, evaluating the pros and cons of each option, and choosing the best possible course of action. Keep in mind that this could be an iterative process.

Being a solution provider at work means that you can help your customers, clients, and stakeholders achieve their goals and overcome their challenges by offering them integrated and customized solutions that meet their needs, and thereby your needs.

59

Communicate your brand.

Brand, Self-awareness, Connection

How do you communicate your professional brand? It's important to know your brand, but do you make it known to others? You can follow this three-step process:

1. Differentiate your brand, know your strengths, and focus on your impact.

2. Share your brand with your manager, colleagues, and teams. You can do this in meetings and in emails, for example, with a clear signature line in your email.

3. Communicate your brand on a regular basis across the media that makes sense for your profession. For example, if it's your LinkedIn profile, have a clear brand statement, a recent professional headshot, and a summary section that includes the impact and influence you have had in your career.

Words on resilience from Resilience Champion Donald Heald

Photo by Cathy Heald

Setting and completing daily and long-term goals contributes to my success and personal fulfillment. For daily tasks, I compile a list of goals by writing them down and then crossing off the tasks once they are achieved. For the few that remained uncrossed, they are moved to the new list for the following day. Looking at the goals that were completed provides a strong feeling of fulfillment and accomplishment. Making lists allows me to clear my mind during the day as I don't worry about trying to remember each specific goal. I apply this to both work and my personal life.

It's important to me to nurture and develop trusting relationships. I am genuinely interested in people and enjoy helping them achieve their goals as best as I can. After the first three years in the pharmaceutical industry, I assumed responsibility for leading large groups of scientists for most of my career. During my first few months in the new leadership position, I will never forget seeing the CEO at Rhone-Poulenc Rorer, a large global Franco-American company with 76,000 employees, walking through the hallways and stopping to chat with colleagues in the hallway, the labs, and their offices. I asked him why a CEO would make time to visit personally with employees. He stated it was very important to him to say "hi," share a smile, shake a hand, and to thank people personally for their efforts.

I quickly realized the value of that and from that time forward, I made the effort to at least twice a year sit down and have an hour-long, face-to-face chat with each colleague in my global groups. It was important for me to get to know each individual, gather feedback and make changes when and where needed, and to understand their career goals. My site heads would meet with me for a two-day meeting twice yearly to talk about every colleague and to determine how best the leadership team could help them achieve their goals. I would make the effort to take groups out for fun dinners or social events. I believe it is important to foster a strong work environment where colleagues have fun working together, which enhances peer-to-peer interactions and leads to the development of trusting relationships among colleagues and leadership. Annual surveys reinforced that this happened.

As I was finishing the demanding research work for my PhD degree, I came across a quote titled "Press On" from Calvin Coolidge, the thirtieth president of the United States, and put it on the second page of my dissertation: "Nothing in this world can take the place of persistence. Talent will not; nothing is more common than unsuccessful men with talent. Genius will not; unrewarded genius is almost a proverb. Education will not; the world is full of educated derelicts. Persistence and determination alone are omnipotent."

The last sentence of the quote describes how I motivate myself to withstand difficulties and accomplish tasks. Regarding career paths, attaining high leadership positions was a long-term goal, but I didn't dwell on how and when this could be achieved. My focus was to work hard on my deliverables, identify and develop new ways to improve large internal cross-functional processes, and develop novel scientific research. These visions were often difficult to attain and there were many substantial barriers and setbacks to overcome. But rather than quitting, which would have been the easy thing to do, I dug deeper, pressed on, found ways to bounce back and to persist and accomplish the goal. I had fun working with others, developing new ideas and solving issues, and in the end to sit back and look at what was accomplished over the years was very rewarding to me.

Recognition for completion of those projects was not sought nor was it my goal, but many wonderful leadership opportunities did come my way. There have been many changes over the years regarding career growth. It is important for scientists to understand and set realistic expectations, timeframes, and understand that hard work, persistence, and determination will lead to recognition, fulfillment, and advancement.

I boost my resilience through prayer and meditation.

When I think of resilience, I think of the words "persistence," "strength," "adaptability," and "determination."

—Donald Heald, PhD
President at Tenacia CP BIO Consulting, LLC

60

Define your professional brand.

Brand

You have unique strengths and skills that make you stand out, characteristics that go beyond your job title—characteristics like problem-solver, teambuilder, or detail-oriented. Your task is to figure out what they are and communicate them in an authentic way.

Your brand should align with having the career reputation you want to have. If someone were talking about you when you were not in the room, what would you like them to say? Try inserting those words in the following: "(Your name) is _____, _____, and _____. That is why I want them involved in this project."

61

Develop your own career board of directors.

Brand, Connection

"Isolation is a dream killer."

—Barbara Sher

If you are going through an important or difficult transition like a career change, gather an informal "board of directors" to help you chart your course. Invite two to four people you trust and admire from family, friends, and business colleagues, treat the group to a special meal, then spend a few hours going over your ideas, brainstorming, or developing an action plan. Be clear on your agenda and make sure you send each person a personalized thank-you and keep all of them posted on your progress.

62

Document your achievements.

Brand, Self-awareness

At the end of every week or once a month, schedule time to write down your career achievements. Ask yourself, "What impact did I make this week or month in my career?" It's important to recognize even small wins as they contribute to building your brand and reputation. This strategy is also useful if your organization has a midyear or annual review. What system can you set up to track your career achievements?

63

Focus on your strengths for a more meaningful life.

Brand, Self-awareness

U sing your strengths in your career is scientifically proven to generate more fulfillment, happiness, and productivity. Make a list of your strengths or take a strength-based assessment.[7]

Try this exercise:

- Write down at least five strengths.

- Put a plus sign next to the ones you are using regularly in your career and personal life.

- Look at any that do not have a positive sign. Can you brainstorm ways to use that strength on a more consistent basis?

---

7   The Values in Action (VIA) Character Strengths Survey is a free online survey used to identify your Values in Action, also known as your character strengths. It's at https://www.viacharacter.org. You'll need to create a VIA Institute account (free and simple to do) to take the quiz.

Words on resilience from Resilience Champion Ashley Milton

I recharge myself by getting outside, either by taking a walk, going for a run, or taking a bike ride. Of course, these activities require me to make the time to do them! But even a thirty-minute stroll has the power to allow my mind to wander and take stock of recent work activities. With work tasks seemingly always building up, I find that by taking a break and allowing my mind to drift, I am more efficient and typically have a better perspective on the task once I return to it.

Deciding to take a day off completely and go cycling often provides me with a real boost. I also remind myself not to take things too seriously; yes, work is important and I want to do my best work, but it should be done by finding the fun within it and seeking a smile or even a laugh with others along the way.

It's important to me to build great relationships in both

my work and personal lives, and I believe that forging trust is one of the most powerful tools for accomplishing this. I try to be as transparent as possible and share my perspectives freely. I am of the view there are very few reasons to keep information secret at work and they are really only for very specific matters (e.g., personal confidentiality or intellectual property). I try to be transparent with pertinent information and have found that giving trust pays you back with interest. We need to build trust and then work to maintain it.

I naturally connect with people. I try to find areas of common interest and time and opportunity to connect with people over them. This has led me to make friends with people I have met through work, and I have even achieved this across geographies and cultures. Once you have this in place, people will often reciprocate and support each other even when work can be challenging.

One piece of advice I'd give to people who want to be more resilient is to recognize that there are often things or events at work or life in general that we don't have any direct control over. It is a good strategy to keep your eyes and ears open and be aware of what transpires around you, but not to become stressed about things that you cannot control.

Be open to new possibilities that can come with such change and be willing to explore them. It is often fear of change that holds us back. I moved countries by being willing to try something new. Then some years later I was made redundant, which was maybe not a total surprise, but it was that change that allowed me time to reflect and decide on what my priorities were. That was when I became more aware of my core values to ensure they were aligned with my next role. I like to remind myself that we should try and find sources of joy in the work we do, but there is always more to life than work alone.

My resilience words are: "adaptable," "consistency," "reliability," and "availability."

—Ashley Milton, PhD
Independent Clinical Pharmacology Consultant

64

Follow up in a mindful way.

Brand

Everyone has experienced the situation of not receiving a response for an extended period of time after an email is sent at work. Instead of stressing over the "why," think about what the regular response style is for the recipient, and follow up accordingly in a respectful way. People may simply miss reading your email, or encounter a computer crash before responding to you even after reading it, or the sent email simply got stuck in the outbox. One useful tip on your side is to inform your colleagues that if they don't hear from you within forty-eight hours (or whatever the time period that routinely works for you), they should feel free to remind you by email or a different communication method that works best for you both. This brings transparency and openness to communication, decreases tension, and can work well when you need to remind others in similar situations.

65

Have a purposeful on-site presence at work.

Brand, Connection

Many organizations operate in a hybrid work arrangement with expectations of on-site presence for a specific number of days per week. Use your days on-site as an opportunity to meet people and engage socially, maximizing in-person connection.

One approach is to set up one-on-one meetings with colleagues who are on-site at the same time you are, while using your work-from-home days to connect with colleagues with whom remote meetings are the only option. There is no point commuting into the office if the day is spent on video calls!

66

Introduce yourself with your brand.

Brand, Connection

Your brand is what makes you memorable. Don't share only your job title at conferences and networking events; share what makes you unique so people will remember you. For example, after giving your title, you can say, "One of my current projects is an online knowledge management system for the company. It involves gathering input from functions company-wide, which is really interesting."

67

Listen actively and practice appreciative inquiry.

Brand, Connection

A ctive listening is a valuable leadership skill. The art of active listening involves engaging actively through body language (e.g., nods, smiles, curious expressions) and via thoughtful questions to seek clarification. Such engagement—without promoting or pushing forward individual points of view or recommendations—will help build trust in team settings. When you're not in sync with a proposal or opinion expressed in a meeting, rather than offering judgment or advocating for an alternate viewpoint or solution, a deliberate inquiry to understand the viewpoint on the table will go a long way in steering not only the proponent but also the entire group in the right direction and enhance acceptance of the right solution.

68

Mitigate your email burden with email etiquette.

Brand, Self-awareness

The volume of email you deal with is significant and has important consequences for your efficiency and effectiveness at work. In addition to being distracting, there is the risk that an important email that requires a follow-up, or contains a time-sensitive or critical communication, can be inadvertently overlooked in a sea of unimportant messages. Maximizing signal-to-noise ratio in email communication is crucial. Here are some tips:

- Do not "reply to all" unless the reply will be meaningful for all recipients.

- Be purposeful in deciding your "To" and "Cc" lists when sending emails. One approach for people you wish to keep informed but protect from the burden of inadvertent or thoughtless subsequent "reply-to-all" messages is to utilize the "Bcc" list. For example, when announcing the promotion, entry, or exit of a colleague from the organization or celebrating a personal or professional milestone, place all intended recipients of such celebratory or announcement emails in Bcc, while including the colleague in focus on the Cc list. This eliminates replies to all recipients while providing the opportunity to reply to the colleague being thanked or celebrated with a personal note. Of course, the writer can also copy the manager or other key stakeholders in their message but still avoiding a "reply to all," which can be quite distracting. The same approach is useful for broadcast messages (e.g., from Facilities, IT, or other such groups) that are intended to inform and are not meant to elicit replies to all.

• A variation of this strategy is that when replying to an email with multiple recipients about an item that is relevant to only some of them (e.g., responding about one project to an email that covers multiple projects), remove the names of people not involved in the project or move their names to Bcc, instead of automatically replying to all.

69

Pay attention to your reputation.

Brand, Self-awareness

Your reputation is an important part of your brand. Think of it this way: What do people say about you when you're not in the room?

Reputation is not static—you can improve it at any time. There are four key factors that can enhance or repair your reputation: competence, connection, commitment, and transparency.

- **Competence** is the knowledge, abilities, skills, and experiences that enable and improve your efficiency and performance.

- **Connection** is the capacity to be proactive and connect with others, understanding what another person is experiencing from within their frame of reference. This is sometimes referred to as putting yourself in the other person's shoes.

- **Commitment** is taking on and fulfilling responsibilities and having clear communication about deadlines and deliverables.

- **Transparency** is operating in a way that is easy for others to see what actions are performed and sharing appropriate information with others.

Focus on your reputation and brand by asking yourself what legacy you want to leave in your life and organization.

Words on resilience from Resilience Champion Sharon J. Swan

eing CEO of an organization brings with it a unique set of expectations. In short, the buck stops with you. With that in mind, I have found that resilience is a mindset. This was engrained in me throughout my early years by my father. I recall from a very young age, he reminded me daily about values and resilience—he referred to it as: "You know what you have to do; don't be deterred by what others think or say. Do the right thing." Throughout my career, I've stuck to my values. I know what they are, and they have guided me, particularly through the tough and challenging times.

You must have absolute clarity on what constitutes success. This is much easier said than done. I have found myself frequently asking staff, members, leaders, and other stakeholders, "Let's clarify: What does success look like?" Asking this question always results in individual introspection and usually brings increased focus to the conversation so that the group can amplify, verify, and clarify exactly what success looks like.

As I reflect on my career, I realize how important resilience was to me. At ASCPT, I worked with twenty-five presidents of the organization. Adjusting your leadership to a new boss (i.e., president) every year requires that you know your values and accept reality and don't sugarcoat it or try to avoid it. You must be willing to adjust your leadership to the situation and always be prepared to take decisive action, focusing always on the best interest of the organization and your members.

Nurturing and developing trusting relationships are key to resilience and begin with ongoing and open communication. In work relationships, building trust is demonstrated by consistently meeting your commitments and promises. In other words, deliver what you have said you would. If circumstances change and other factors get in the way of meeting your commitment or promise, immediately reach out to the individual(s) to whom you promised a deliverable and explain the situation, noting clearly when you will deliver what you have promised.

In my work with ASCPT, building trust with staff, members, leaders, and other stakeholders is essential in relationship building. Trustworthiness also involves candor and sharing perspectives. We know that trust builds slowly and consistently over time, so it is important to continually demonstrate trustworthiness in what you do. This was never more evident than during the recent COVID-19 pandemic when many associations and non-profits were forced to cancel in-person meetings and events, often their largest source of revenue. It also necessitated renegotiating contracts with vendors. Many days I found myself digging very deep to explain the gravity of the situation and the ripple effect that the pandemic had on associations. Irrespective of our cause, associations are in the people business. The trust you build through relationships with members, member leaders, stakeholders, and staff over many years really pays dividends when times are tough and difficult decisions need to be made.

My thoughts on trust conclude with this quote by Brené Brown from *The Gifts of Imperfection*: "I define connection as the energy that exists between people when they feel seen, heard, and valued; when they can give and receive without judgment; and when they derive sustenance and strength from the relationship."

My daily resilience habit is using the Calm app to help me reduce stress and improve focus. It has transformed my life. I use mindful breathing techniques multiple times throughout the day. Using the app helps me fall asleep faster, and, when awakened during the night, the breathing techniques assist me in getting back to sleep. With use of the app, I am able to clear my head of distracting thoughts and to let negative thoughts, comments, and feedback roll off me. Further, I am much less burdened by the pressures and distractions of the day, as my mind is clear.

I began using the app in 2018 and since then have done more than 4,408 total sessions on the app. This translates into more than 1,368 hours. My longest consecutive streak using the app was 403 days. Since my retirement at the end of 2022, I have continued to use the Calm app daily.

I like this quote by Jaeda Dewalt, a photographic artist, writer, and poet: "When we learn how to become resilient, we learn how to embrace the beautifully broad spectrum of the human experience."

Lastly, a note about personal and professional balance. This is far easier said than done. With the responsibilities of being CEO, the staff and members depend on you to always be on top of your game. To sustain yourself in a key leadership role, it takes discipline and a focus on your health and well-being. While healthy eating has always been a part of my life, my exercise regimen was on-again, off-again. Early in my CEO role, the needs of the organization took much of my time and attention. Once the organization was on solid footing with staff and capable volunteer leadership, I made the time to devote to my physical and mental well-being with a rigorous exercise program. As they say on the airplane, in case of a loss of cabin pressure, put on your own mask first, then help others traveling with you.

I conclude my thoughts on resilience, career success, and a fulfilled life with the following quote by Angela Duckworth from *Grit: The Power of Passion and Perseverance*: "Enthusiasm is common. Endurance is rare."

The three words I associate with resilience are: "prioritization," "self-acceptance," and "calm."

—Sharon J. Swan, FASAE, CAE
Principal, Swan Advisors, CEO Emeritus, American
Society for Clinical Pharmacology & Therapeutics (ASCPT)

70

Project confidence, calm, and professionalism when faced with difficult situations at work.

Brand, Self-awareness

You might have experienced a situation when a co-worker lost their temper and professionalism during a group meeting, which led to an undesirable outcome, including not finding solutions to a problem and reduced work morale. Being resilient means that you can minimize such behaviors despite having the urge to indulge in them. It also means that you stay professional by handling challenges with grace, respect, and composure. Importantly, be empathetic by putting yourself in others' shoes as many difficult situations arise from the human factors and emotions being affected.

71

Show empathy and respect for work–life balance in email communications.

Brand, Self-awareness

When sending emails, recognize the impact of sending them during after-work hours for the recipient. Mindfulness with the timing of emails is particularly crucial in global settings across very different time zones (e.g., Asia and the Americas). Sending an email in the morning from the Americas could result in it being received during or after dinner time in East Asia, leading to the unintended consequence of the colleague feeling pressured to reply or engage in the dialogue that ensues. Include a statement in the signature block along the lines of "I value and support flexible working and acknowledge that your working hours may be different from mine. While this message was sent during a time that works best for me, please do not feel obligated to read and reply outside of your normal working schedule." If replies within a timeframe are expected from certain recipients, it is best to clarify this in the message and as needed in the subject line.

Another strategy is to schedule the delivery time of the email to avoid sending emails at night or over the weekend. It is understandable that you may be doing some work occasionally after dinner or on a Saturday or Sunday that involves email communication. Rather than hitting "Send" right away, set the delivery to a time that is within normal working hours.

These strategies may not work for everyone all the time, but mindfulness and respect for others in email communications are crucial to enabling work-life balance and sustaining a resilient organization.

72

Volunteer your time and talent.

Brand, Connection, Innovation

Culturally, we are often taught to absorb as much as we can and even take more than we really need. We forget that the essence of happiness lies in creating an ecosystem of giving back, starting from ourselves. Here are some ideas:

- At work, if your department offers rotation opportunities for others not in your area of expertise, be proactive in taking on those mentor roles and help those who may want to expand their horizons for new job opportunities.

- Within your department or company, create a thirty- to sixty-minute tutorial or introduction about your field for those who are not familiar with your specialty. This may trigger conversations, collaborations, and opportunities for you and others, which can lead to innovation and enhanced connectivity.

- More broadly, teach a skill that you have mastered to someone who wants to learn it. You can offer your expertise in areas like fitness, finance, public speaking, sports, art, horticulture, or home repairs to local community centers, schools, or individuals.

- Volunteer online from the comfort of your own home—you can find virtual volunteer opportunities that match your interests and skills on platforms like VolunteerMatch.

- Do a few chores for someone who needs help. Offer to cut the grass, rake the leaves, prepare meals, or walk the dog for a friend, family member, or neighbor who is busy, elderly, or disabled. No offering is too small, and small endeavors create wonders of massive scale, such as a better working and living environment for everyone.

- Volunteer for a community organization that supports a cause you believe in or share your career insights at a high school or college career event. Many students can benefit from your career wisdom.

continued

Volunteering is a great way to give back and learn about different organizations that could benefit from your assistance.

True to my passion for storytelling and writing, which were nurtured by my mother, Shantha Venkatakrishnan, and later on by my PhD advisor, Professor David Greenblatt, I volunteer my time to peer review and serve on editorial boards of scientific journals in my discipline. I additionally contribute as a volunteer leader and mentor in professional organizations. These experiences have broadened my network of mentors, collaborators, and mentees, enabling my resilience via connection, innovation, and continuous evolution of my professional brand.

—**Karthik Venkatakrishnan**

73

Bring more fun and joy into your workday.

Connection, Brand

Begin department meetings with an icebreaker. Share a fun question, recent vacation photo, or favorite cartoon. Take time to connect with your team before focusing on your agenda item. By having fun, you stay creative, reduce stress, and improve trust with co-workers and collaboration with customers.

My husband, Patrick, has a manager who leads his department in a stop-and-stretch activity for fifteen minutes once a week on their video call. It's a simple way to take a mini-break, have fun, and recharge, and I enjoy hearing the laughter from his team.

—Beth Kennedy

Words on resilience
from Resilience Champion
Gayle Draper

Photo by Ben Frisch, BFresh Media

As a career transition coach, I work with a wide range of people with very diverse occupations. I share and encourage them to follow a daily habit I have. Each time I wash my hands throughout the day, I take an extra five seconds, cup my hands, and ask myself, "Did something fill this cup with positive energy or did something deplete this cup?" It may be the work I did, the people I was with, or the situation I was in. This self-check throughout the day reminds me to replenish myself all through the day and not wait to find time at the end of the day. It may be a micro-break, a nutrition break, being outside with my dog, or five minutes to recognize some emotions.

These self-check-ins determine how I spend my breaks. My MBTI personality type is ENFP, so this may be:

- A specific friend to restore my high extraverted (E) energy level

- A vision exercise to exercise my intuition (N) to focus on the bigger picture

- A walk in the park to reflect or process my high feelings (F)

- Something spontaneous to acknowledge my high needs (P) giving myself time with no list and great autonomy

Another important aspect of my resilience is nurturing trusting relationships. In earlier chapters of my career, I always had a goal of a weekly conversation with a past co-worker or friend to keep my network nurtured. This was an opportunity for me to keep in contact with people, foster our relationships, and offer my support or help if needed.

I still have that approach, but I have also built a dragon boat filled with people I trust, especially during those times when things in my personal or professional life present more of a challenge. I always encourage clients to never be solo in a kayak but to build a dragon boat filled with people with different strengths and experiences that are a call away for advice and encouragement, a new approach to a challenge, or confirmation of a strategy. All my dragon boat members have proven from past experiences that they believe in peer support, have a value system that aligns with mine, and have a lifelong learning philosophy that they are eager to share and receive.

One piece of advice that I would give people who want to be more resilient in their career or life is to use the

Benatti Resiliency Model to focus on the five critical areas of self-awareness, brand, connection, innovation, and well-being. All are essential and work in harmony.

One of my biggest career challenges was to begin Intentional Careers HR at age fifty. I had always wanted to do this and needed a mindset that would fuel positive forward momentum during the challenging early days as a solopreneur and all the bumps along the way. My mindset is to look at moving through challenges with the four Ps:

1. Be Positive with your approach and relationships.

2. Be Proactive to create and develop your opportunities.

3. Be a Planner to look at different paths to get to your end goals.

4. Be Prepared for what should and may happen.

The words that come to mind when I think of resilience are: "bounce-ability," "self-awareness," and "nutritional fuel."

—Gayle Draper
Career Transition Specialist

74

Connect outside your discipline.

Connection, Innovation, Brand

Ideate, establish connections, and forge collaborations beyond the borders of your own discipline and sector of practice to help address problems. This generates diversity of thought and options for solutions from multiple perspectives, making the resulting solutions more versatile and sustainable. Importantly, you learn from others in multidisciplinary collaborations, especially when they transcend sectors of practice (e.g., industry, government, education, consulting). You'll make friends who share your orientation to a common purpose but with a different knowledge base, skill set, and life experience, enriching your self-awareness and enabling progressive evolution of your personal and professional brand.

One example of such a connection is between the three authors—Beth, Ben, and Karthik—who came together with a passion for sharing their strategies to boost resilience, fueled by their own distinct experiences in their careers and across sectors of practice.

75

Connect regularly with individuals "in your boat."

Connection

When you're swamped by a long to-do list on a daily basis, nurturing mutually beneficial relationships that expand your network, effectiveness, and helpfulness in professional settings can be challenging. If you find calendar reminders useful for regular tasks and meetings, why not try putting down recurring reminders for checking in with those who are "in your boat." This doesn't mean you are obligated to do anything with that individual on those days. Instead, the reminder can serve as a placeholder for you to have a reflection on whether there are meaningful updates to provide on your end. Importantly, even if there is nothing substantial to share, saying hi can still be important, particularly if you can provide help and support in times of need. Overall, connecting with others can boost your mood, reduce stress, improve self-esteem, and contribute to living longer and having a better quality of life.

76

Create boundaries with toxic people.

Connection, Well-being

A n important part of recharge is staying away from or minimizing contact with the toxic people in your life. Toxic individuals will not build your resilience, just increase your stress and drain your energy.

Common types of toxic people include:

- **The grouches.** These are people who are chronically unhappy, pessimistic, or irritable.

- **The energy vampires.** These are people for whom everything is about them. You will notice that they never ask anything about you.

- **The drama kings and queens.** These are people who are addicted to drama and turn every work or personal conflict into a soap opera for which you have to play audience.

Life is too short to spend time with people who deplete you. Be aware of how you feel when you're with others. Ask yourself if they revitalize you or exhaust you when you spend time with them. If it's the latter, set clear boundaries with them.

77

Engage in mentoring relationships.

Connection, Innovation, Brand

Offer to be a mentor for students and early career professionals. Mentoring fosters connection and self-confidence. Mentors can learn from mentees as well, making it a win-win engagement, thereby enhancing one's professional brand. Mentoring need not be via formal assignment of mentor/mentee roles in organized mentorship programs; it can be nurtured organically as a relationship between two individuals with complementary skills or strengths or at different stages of their career journeys.

78

Have a confidant.

Connection

t is important to have individuals in whom you can con-
fide and openly share your lows, insecurities, and regrets.
We all experience times when we feel we did not quite
meet our own expectations or let someone down or weren't
at our best when something was important. Rather than
ruminating in isolation, have people who can listen without
being judgmental but can also provide realistic and balanced
reassurance, as well as insights that help you learn from the
experience. Being able to reach out and say, "I need to speak
with you," and share openly without fear of judgment is vital
to well-being. Pay it forward by being there in a similar way
for another person (and it need not necessarily be the same
person you lean on).

Words on resilience from Resilience Champion Alexandra S. Zappala

Photo by Brian Zappala Jr.

T o focus on resilience is to reframe our perspective: to emphasize passion, purpose, hope, perseverance, and effort rather than the "limits" of our innate talents and abilities. Say you were born with a genius-level IQ, the frame of a natural athlete, or the singing voice of an angel. None of those abilities amount to anything without effort and resilience. I have found myself many times in life comparing my ability to others, dwelling on why certain things are more difficult for me, and feeling defeated by my shortcomings and failures. That's okay, and of course it is important to honor our emotions, but I have found success in responding by using that as fuel for my passion, a reminder of my determination and purpose, and a challenge to keep pushing forward.

The practice of meeting with a mentor has been, and continues to be, one of the most important aspects of my professional and personal development. In my opinion, nobody accomplishes anything entirely on their own. Even with all the right attributes—hard work, passion, perseverance—the power of support cannot be emphasized enough. I can confidently say that I would not be where I am today without the support and guidance of mentors. As clinical psychology graduate trainees, we were required to attend a weekly clinical supervision, time to meet with supervisors and mentors to discuss cases, clinical work, professional development, and our personal development. Many psychologists, including myself, choose to continue this weekly practice even when their formal training is complete. This speaks to the benefits derived from the support of mentors. My mentors serve as role models, allies, and gentle critics; they offer encouragement, empathy, wisdom, and insight. I am so grateful for their support, guidance, and impact on my success and personal fulfillment.

I would advise people who want to be more resilient to learn from their failures so they can adjust their course and give themselves a chance to try again. It is important to fail—there is no such thing as true success without some degree of failure along the way—and it's important to remember our humility so that we never stop striving for better. I would advise others to embrace failure as developmental feedback and an opportunity to exercise resilience. Struggle and failure are inevitable, so let them add to the richness and meaning of your journey.

The words that come to mind when I hear the word "resilience" are: "grit," "hope," "purpose," and "courage."

—Alexandra S. Zappala, PsyD
Staff Psychologist, Villanova University Counseling Center

79

Leave room for having non-forced fun with your co-workers.

Connection

It's important to get one's job done, but try to leave room to have non-forced fun with your co-workers without taking away valuable time outside of work. This can help build rapport, trust, and camaraderie, as well as reduce stress, boost morale, and nurture creativity. There are numerous ways of doing this. For example, form an office or department sports team, create a relaxation or gaming area in your workplace, host "fancy" or "ugly" clothing days where you dress up in costumes or themes, or go out together as a team. Since many of us spend a lot of time in professional work settings with others, it makes sense to get to know our co-workers by having engaging personal interactions with them and focusing more on what we can do in the office to enhance communication. In this way, extracurricular activities do not become a burden and can be more enriching.

80

Make a connection when traveling.

Connection

Traveling (whether for work or leisure) does not have to be done alone, even when you are going somewhere by yourself. Take the opportunity to get to know the person sitting next to you in the airplane. These connections can make traveling fun and infuse anticipation and fulfillment that goes beyond the core purpose of the trip. If you plan an evening of sightseeing and decide to go on a tour, introduce yourself to and speak with people with whom you are sharing an exploration trail, boat ride, or other activity; this can open up new connections.

On my way back to Boston from Germany after a recent business trip, I had the pleasure of an engaging conversation with the person seated next to me who lived in the Munich area and was traveling to a business meeting in Boston. Not only did this make the eight-hour flight more enjoyable, but we also realized that we shared some interests, including a passion for international travel and tourism, and common items on our bucket lists! We have since stayed in touch via WhatsApp messaging and exchanged photographs taken during subsequent travels.

—Karthik Venkatakrishnan

81

Approach artificial intelligence (AI) with curiosity.

Innovation

With the explosive increases in the development and application of artificial intelligence (e.g., generative AI) in everyday work and in specialized sectors of practice, we encourage our readers to be curious and open to embracing this emerging technology with the possibility that it will maximize productivity, efficiency, and competitiveness.

Talk to an AI-based chatbot or search engine and you may be pleasantly surprised how much they can help you boost your resilience. While it is important to recognize the caveats of responses generated by AI, one may still benefit greatly by conducting mindful "conversations" and searches with

AI-based tools, especially when they open the doors to new ideas and possibilities.

If you are not an early adopter, don't worry—it is never too late to try!

Image created by Songmao to illustrate the concept for the AI-generated photo, using "A resilient person embraces life" at https://deepai.org/machine-learning-model/text2img.

82

Be inclusive and enable a diverse work setting.

Innovation, Self-awareness

Surround yourself with people who are different from you. When interviewing people for open positions on your team, don't try to find people who are similar to you, but aim to build a team with diverse experiences, perspectives, and interpersonal styles. Diversity brings strength to a team and elevates quality of thought and innovation, thereby enhancing influence and impact. To maximize the likelihood of building a diverse team, increase the diversity of your interview panel. Building and leading a team of like-minded individuals is a path of low resistance and might be more comfortable and fulfilling in the short-term, but the long-term benefits of actively nurturing diversity of opinion are substantial. Diversity can enable a team to successfully identify and solve problems that haven't been previously solved, elevating the team's performance to new heights at the enterprise level.

83

Be proactive in exploring and interviewing for new job opportunities.

Innovation, Brand, Self-awareness

B e purposeful about the process of identifying job openings that warrant evaluation even if you're content in your current job. While such exploration should not distract from your commitment to your current job or generate stress and confusion, investing time in evaluating relevant opportunities that might be the right next step in your career journey is an important part of a proactive approach to professional development. It's easy to get comfortable in the demands of your current job to the point where you lose sight of external opportunities for career advancement.

The process of going through an interview can boost self-esteem, enhance a critical understanding of self-worth, and enable appreciation of the positives in one's current job even if the going gets tough during times of change, excessive workload, or uncertainty. Such an experience can foster self-reflection regarding the scope and impact of your current role and the need for continuing education in emerging areas. This can inform development conversations with one's manager that may pave the way for broadening your current role or expanding development paths.

84

Break large tasks into doable pieces.

Innovation, Well-being

A good strategy to boost your resilience and productivity is to break bigger tasks into doable pieces. This can help you avoid procrastination and keep you from feeling overwhelmed and losing focus and motivation. Some recommended steps:

- Identify the main goal of your task and why it is important.

- Divide the main goal into sub-goals that are smaller, more specific, and more manageable.

- Assign a deadline and a priority level to each sub-goal.

- Specify the resources and tools needed to enable these sub-goals, as well as potential gaps and roadblocks.

- Use your calendar to schedule when these sub-tasks should be completed while building in buffer time to allow for unexpected scenarios.

- Track progress and document your successes and learnings.

Keep in mind that not every task can or should be broken into pieces as too many pieces could be distracting. Being flexible, agile, and adaptable about what it takes to get things done is equally important.

85

Explore continuous learning opportunities.

Innovation

A ctively take advantage of continuous learning opportunities. This can range from listening to webinars and inspirational podcasts to watching YouTube presentations to signing up for LinkedIn Learning. When registering for these, block off the time on your calendar and protect it to ensure commitment to, and benefit from, the learning activity.

I have a few colleagues with whom I meet informally once a month to share learnings from webinars we have watched and discuss takeaways from professional books we are reading. It keeps me accountable and innovative and helps me process what I learn.

—Beth Kennedy

86

Get spontaneous.

Innovation, Well-being

Many of us are oriented toward a controlled and regimented lifestyle, planning and organizing activities ahead of time. That may come at a cost as linear life paths void of spontaneity and irregularities can leave you feeling dull, empty, uninspired, unmotivated, and burned out. It's as if you're checking off boxes in your life, constantly hoping and preparing for the next best thing. Spontaneity can potentially trigger new ideas, inspiration, and relaxation and refresh your ways of thinking, as well as of execution. Occasionally tearing up your usual schedule in favor of spontaneity can lead to new possibilities and beginnings. Research has shown that acting without a plan (i.e., spontaneity) can increase happiness, vitality, and fulfillment.[8] Spontaneity could rejuvenate your life!

> I decided four hours before the plane left to attend the 2023 Tamiami International Orchid Festival and did not regret it for one second because of the conversations I had, the old friends I met and new friends I made, and the knowledge obtained through chatting with people who had over twenty years of growing experience. I also obtained some unique orchids from around the world.
>
> **—Songmao (Ben) Zheng**

---

8   Katina Bajaj, "Routines Are Great, but Spontaneity Is the Key to Brain Expansion—Here's Why," *mbghealth* (blog), January 24, 2023, https://www.mindbodygreen.com/articles/why-being-spontaneous-is-key-to-mental-health.

87

Practice financial planning to allow you to enjoy life.

Innovation, Self-awareness, Well-being

Financial planning is often aimed at buying a home, education of children, and investment for retirement. While these are critically important reasons to plan your finances, it is important to also plan for enjoyable experiences. You have one life to live, so don't wait too long to do the things on your bucket list. For example, if you'd like to plan a physically demanding trek, it might be better done a bit earlier in life rather than holding off until retirement.

Planning thoughtfully to enjoy life to the fullest is an important component of recharging for resilience. Whether it is the pleasure of being in the front row of a concert of your favorite band in an amazing venue at the opposite end of the world or something more ambitious like space tourism, there is no harm in dreaming big and planning with realistic boundaries and expectations to help realize the dreams that matter without breaking the bank.

Words on resilience from Resilience Champion Brent A. Hackett

Resilience is all about flexibility. In my career, I have worn many hats and, despite never feeling fully prepared to take on any of these roles at the outset, I persisted and found success. To that end, a bend-but-don't-break mentality has been a key feature. I try to keep as few "red lines" as possible and remain willing to take on new things, even when they aren't exactly within my purview. Going with the flow in this manner has also been great because when I become aware that I am crossing a red line, I know that it is a serious breach that needs attention. I also try, where possible, to import this professional philosophy into personal relationships, which I hope makes me a bit more tolerant and understanding of others' unique qualities.

A resilience habit that contributes to my success and personal fulfillment is making it a point to learn something new (and outside the scope of my work) every week. For me, this tends to favor history or art, but the subject matter can be tailored to any number of personal interests and may be as simple as watching a documentary on YouTube or reading a news article. Because being a lifelong learner is such an essential part of resilience, sharpening one's mind through the continuous picking up of new bits of information is a great way to maintain plasticity and become more well-rounded. Besides, you never know when a random fact can be the nexus to a new connection or opportunity. It has been the case for me on more than a few occasions.

To be more resilient, stay humble but know your worth. Humility has played a huge part in my journey and has been a trait that has served me well over years of precarious or stopgap situations. However, humility does not merely equate to taking what one is given; instead, it concerns the understanding that there will always be more to know and improvements to be made. In short, if you ever find yourself merely trumpeting your credentials (no matter how well-earned) and thinking that this alone is enough, then I would suggest that you have either (1) sold yourself short and should be aiming higher or (2) are not as secure as you may think.

My three resilience words are: "grit," "adaptability," and "flexibility."

—Brent A. Hackett, PhD, Esq.
Patent Counsel, Sarepta Therapeutics

88

If what you're doing now isn't working, try doing something else.

Innovation

I f you want to change your results, change your actions. Doing the same thing over and over and expecting a different result is not effective or efficient. Experiment with possible changes in direction, backed by rationales and data. If you identify something that is constantly leading to undesirable outcomes, be analytical and come up with executable activities. Even with incremental changes, you are on the trajectory of a more favorable outcome.

Remember, making big changes is hard, but making smaller, manageable changes over an extended period of time is more feasible. Being comfortable with being a bit uncomfortable is the way to go!

89

Infuse variety in daily activities.

Innovation, Self-awareness

Using the same brand, flavor, or fragrance of toothpaste, soap, shampoo, or deodorant daily may be necessary for health reasons (e.g., allergy to specific fragrances or ingredients), but when no such constraints exist, trying out new brands or flavors and fragrances can add variety to daily activities and spark a level of mindfulness that can be rejuvenating. For example, if you have a few different flavors of toothpaste on hand, the simple decision of whether to start your day with peppermint-, wintergreen-, or cinnamon-clove-flavored toothpaste can add mindful enjoyment of the task of brushing your teeth. This can give you a zing of energy that comes from reacting to this simple selection and the associated gustatory experience of what is otherwise taken for granted as a mundane activity of daily living.

90

Learn a new language.

Innovation, Connection

earning a new language can spark curiosity and creativity and foster an innovative spirit. Research shows that learning a new language can improve memory, concentration, and attention span and may even help enhance cognition.[9]

It can also enable connection with a range of people across cultures and geography and enhance flexibility and perspective, which contributes to both a broadening of career options across geographies and a more connected and fulfilled life.

In addition, the positive reinforcement that results from this learning experience will enhance your self-esteem and nurture a can-do mindset in all areas of life, including, but not limited to, your primary professional sector of practice.

---

9   Angelika Pokovba, "Need a New Hobby? Learning Another Language Is like Fitness Training for Your Brain," *Real Simple*, January 26, 2024, https://www.realsimple.com/cognitive-benefits-of-learning-second-language-7109650.

91

Make Sunday fun day.

Innovation, Well-being

It is easy to end up spending the weekend on chores or work that still needs to get done. Before you know it, Monday is here, and you are back to focusing on work again. Plan something fun every Sunday, and plan what you will do the following weekend. The anticipation will power you through the workweek. Don't wait till you have free time to do something fun—you may never feel like you have enough free time.

I coach individuals who are very passionate about their careers but often have difficulty setting boundaries so they can rest and recharge on the weekends. I often give this Resiliency Booster as a homework assignment to these clients. After it becomes a habit, they love it and notice the positive impact it has on their career and life.

—Beth Kennedy

92

Narrow virtual distances despite working remotely.

Innovation, Connection

I t's easy to lose touch with people: We're "too busy" or we're overwhelmed by information and noise. We send texts every now and then but don't meet in person as often as before and feel more isolated than ever. Flexible working styles, including remote working some or all of the time, have become the norm for many in the post-pandemic era. Consequently, forming strong working relationships can be challenging.

Besides utilizing opportunities to meet and greet people on-site, try these techniques to narrow the virtual distances:

- Be more intentional in acknowledging and celebrating other people's successes and achievements (e.g., nominating others for internal or external awards, expressing appreciation during meetings).

- Mail a token of appreciation for a colleague's efforts, one that is customized to the preference of the individual. Some organizations have programs that facilitate giving gift cards.

- Mail a postcard when you travel or send one through a service that lets you use your own pictures.

- Host online events such as coffee breaks or lunch and focus on nonwork-related topics.

Genuine human connection is a remedy to isolation and loneliness, even virtually.

93

Opt for a secondment.

Innovation

aking a secondment, which may be structured as a job rotation or temporary assignment, as part of your development plan can be a valuable way to gain knowledge, skills, and experience in new areas within one's organization. The variety of experiences and interdisciplinary learning that come from such assignments can pave the way for innovation and broadening one's leadership development. For example, a scientist may benefit from a secondment in project management, and a research and development professional may benefit from a secondment in the commercial sector. Such experiential assignments can be a valuable investment of time, both for the individual and the organization.

94

Play tourist where you live.

Innovation, Well-being

For many people, travel sparks curiosity and creativity. They notice interesting details because they are looking at their surroundings differently. They experience fun and joy from the unexpected.

However, you don't have to leave home to reap the benefits of travel. Instead, try being a tourist where you live. In your daily life, it's easy to get caught up in traveling the same routes to work, school, and the grocery store, eating at the same restaurants, and going to the same movie theater or art museum when you have leisure time.

Try seeing your hometown from the standpoint of a tourist. Look at a travel site online and see what attractions there are that you've never explored. While you're there, look for restaurants you haven't tried. You could even book a night at a hotel in a part of town you don't usually visit and have the fun of waking up someplace different and eating breakfast in a café instead of your own kitchen.

Photos taken by Beth, Karthik, and Songmao when they played tourist where they live.

Words on resilience from Resilience Champion Parag Mallick

Photo by Dougal Brownlie, courtesy of Nautilus Biotechnology

When I think about recharge, I find it helpful to think in the context of my day-to-day life. I love growing my company and leading a fantastic research team at Stanford, but I need to balance the structure and types of wins I get from work with my recharge activities. The three main things I find the need to balance are:

1. My life is overscheduled from dawn to dawn.

2. My colleagues and I are working toward world-changing goals that take years of concerted effort. That being the case, these are delayed-gratification activities. Furthermore, intermediate wins might not be very tangible. For example, on the technical side, I might make a chart or a graph that is highly effective at communicating an exciting result while, on the

non-technical side, I might help resolve a conflict or help a team member achieve their goals. These are great wins, but you can't touch and feel them, and they might not directly contribute to the happiness of a person or group of people—something I find particularly fulfilling.

3. At heart, I'm a creative. It's important for me to balance the technical with the artistic.

Consequently, the most recharging activities for me are ones that are relatively unbounded, creative, and have immediate, tangible outcomes. I've also found it critical to nurture my sense of play and find activities that induce a flow state. That state of play and flow provides a sense of freedom in my largely scheduled life. As a result, my most effective recharges come from extracurricular, artistic projects with defined end points.

From the past year, I have two great examples of these kinds of recharge activities:

1. Making an anniversary present for my wife. For our two-year anniversary, I decided to make my wife an animation of a moment from our relationship in the look and feel of a classic *Super Mario Bros.* video game. Though I have a lot of experience in graphic design, I have *none* in animation. The project had lots of intermediate wins that were concrete: from the initial character design, to the graphics for each scene, and ultimately to the video itself. By the end, I'd produced

something very tangible, on a short timeline, and it brought my wife joy. During the process, there were many moments of flow, where I was caught up in the act of creation.

2. Making a new magic act. For context, I have a side-hustle as a professional magician, and I'd been booked to perform at a fundraiser for a local non-profit foundation. Because of some of the technical requirements of the event and venue, my typical act wouldn't work. Consequently, I had to build one from scratch. The process of creating a new routine is both intense and exhilarating. There are wins along the way as you define an arc for the act, decide which effects to include, discover how to link them together through patter and storyline, and sift through a thousand details of presentation. It's tremendous fun being lost in the process. The payoff is huge—bringing joy to an audience and supporting a good cause.

These projects recharged me immensely, and along-side them, I've found routines also help build resilience. Importantly, routines can themselves become draining if they just end up becoming new boxes to tick. I try to leave routines behind if they become work. Nonetheless, one routine has become critical for me: breakfast (or tea) in front of my kitchen sink.

At first, this might seem like a terrible resilience habit. After all, eating breakfast while standing, or on your way out the door, is almost exactly what smart people tell you *not* to do. Additionally, the kitchen sink is not typically the most glamorous of locations to have breakfast. On the other hand, what I've found is this activity is easy to do, forces me to start my day by slowing down instead of accelerating and rushing out the door, and gives me a moment of calm before the storm of my day. Also, I have a great kitchen window. It looks out over the bay and just feels serene. I don't think the view actually matters much, but it's a location that I associate with tranquility. There is a magical bubble in front of my kitchen sink and standing there for even five minutes drinking my tea or my protein shake helps center me. It builds a bit of a shield against the chaos of my day and also gives me a moment for reflection and gratitude, which I believe are helpful in driving fulfillment.

Parallel to these activities, and just as important for recharge and resilience, I make sure to develop trusting relationships in my work and life. I do so by not overthinking it. I don't set out tasks to explicitly create those relationships. Instead, I focus on defining a set of beliefs, values, and principles for myself and on living my life authentically in support of those beliefs, values, and principles.

For example, I believe that every single person matters and has a valuable perspective. Once you truly embrace that belief, a series of actions follows: listening to people to understand their perspective, trying to help them, and recognizing the uniqueness of each individual in front of you instead of reducing them to a statistic.

People can tell when you are manipulating them. People can tell when you don't care and are faking it. People can tell when you aren't really paying attention to them. Don't fake it. Just work on yourself to understand your beliefs and then live those beliefs.

By treating people well as a matter of course, I organically develop relationships that are fulfilling and surround myself with people who support one another when recharge is needed. This support is absolutely critical for resilience.

The words that come into my mind when I hear "resilience" are: "necessary," "difficult," and "athletes" (because they spend as much effort on rest and recovery as training and execution).

—Parag Mallick, PhD
Associate Professor, Stanford University
Founder and Chief Scientist, Nautilus Biotechnology

95

Practice timeboxing.

Innovation, Well-being

Many jobs require reviewing documents, preparation of slide decks for presentations, scholarship and literature research in advance of a think tank session, or pre-reading in readiness for meetings. With many such tasks on top of a day of meetings, you could be left with little time for life outside of work or even for a short break for lunch or dinner, ending up with fourteen-hour workdays that leave you exhausted and compromise the quality of your work and well-being.

Timeboxing is a valuable technique in which you allocate a fixed amount of time to a planned activity and hold yourself accountable to working on it with undivided attention and focus during that time. Define your rules and resist the temptation to open emails or instant messages when working on a timeboxed activity. Set a timer at one or more points during the time period (e.g., at 45 minutes for a 90-minute timeboxed activity and another when time is almost up, say at 10 minutes ahead of the end) to assess progress against the goal and course-correct your pace and focus. At the end of the boxed time, move on to the next item on your agenda for the day (even if it's just a block of time for a meal or to take a walk to recharge), resisting the temptation to continue with the timeboxed activity. Critical to the success of the timeboxing approach is holding yourself accountable while being realistic in defining an appropriate amount of time for each activity you decide to timebox.

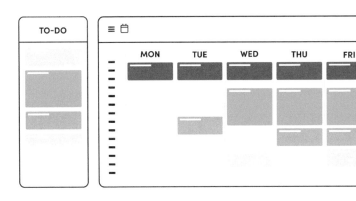

96

Set aside approximately 10 percent of your work time for innovation.

Innovation, Brand

You can often feel buried in seemingly endless routine tasks, with no flexibility or freedom to innovate within the scope of your work. The danger of being swallowed up by such repetitive activities is that you lose sight of opportunities that can propel you toward the next frontier.

Once you understand your core working tasks and priorities based on organizational goals and objectives, take time to ask questions and explore how to set aside time for the "above-and-beyond" type of challenge. It is never too bold to inquire about what is on the horizon and what is important for the next three to five years, no matter what your position is. The exact percentages to be allocated to such innovations will vary over time, and should be agreed upon with key stakeholders so that there is not only room for innovation, but also the platform to demonstrate the impact of these innovations. Ultimately, investing time and energy in these activities can rejuvenate your passion for work and help prevent burnout.

97

Take a cross-regional or international assignment.

Innovation, Brand, Self-awareness

Take the opportunity for a cross-cultural or international assignment when working for a multinational organization—it's a valuable experience. Living abroad and working cross-culturally can enrich your brand as a flexible, inclusive, and empathetic leader. Even if your organization is not global, take opportunities for international travel to conferences and workshops as part of your professional development; it can enhance self-awareness and leadership development.

98

Take time for professional innovation.

Innovation, Connection

t is gratifying to learn a new competency or master an existing skill. Taking this step on the path to greater career fulfillment opens a world of possibilities. If you have the bandwidth, ask to be involved in an interesting work project or offer to serve on a committee. You may even find getting involved in a professional organization for your career area provides a wonderful opportunity to connect with other motivated, like-minded career professionals, which can be energizing.

99

Share your stories and perspectives through writing.

Well-being, Self-awareness, Brand, Connection, Innovation

Spread the word; write for others to read. The process of writing—whether it's a short perspective in a journal, a larger content-rich piece such as a column for a local newspaper or newsletter, or an entire book—can stimulate discovery, cultivate patience, and foster discipline. Having a published work product that is read by others can be a very rewarding experience. Partnering with others to do this can be even more rewarding.

Writing *ReThink Resilience* was a fun way for the three authors to meet regularly, develop a closer friendship, and make a difference in others' lives. Having co-authors made a project that could be isolating more interesting and stimulating and was a great recharge.

Word cloud generated from the authors' first joint publication where they surveyed professionals on LinkedIn with an open-ended question: "Please describe one thing that you find most useful to boost your resilience."[10]

---

10 Songmao Zheng, Karthik Venkatakrishnan, and Beth Benatti Kennedy, "How Resilient Were We in 2021? Results of a LinkedIn Survey Including Biomedical and Pharmaceutical Professionals Using the Benatti Resiliency Model," *Clinical and Translational Science* 15, no. 10 (August 2022): 2355–2365, https://doi.org/10.1111/cts.13364.

How to Make a
Habit of Resilience

Y ou've read through the boosters. One or more reso-
nated with you. Now what? How do you incorporate
a resilience booster into your life? In other words, how
do you make resilience a habit?

Three Strategies to Create a Habit

1. Start small. Keep your goals as small as possible when
developing a new habit. The smaller you make the
first action step, the greater overall success you will
have. B. J. Fogg, a Stanford psychologist, has done
extensive research that demonstrates that goal-setting
often creates stress rather than being productive.
Fogg believes that changing behavior is not just about
getting motivated; it's also about making the initial
behavior change easy to accomplish.[11]

---

11   Lila MacLellan, "A Stanford University Psychologist's Elegant Three-Step
Method for Creating New Habits," *Quartz*, January 4, 2017, https://qz.com
/877795/how-to-create-new-good-habits-according-to-stanford
-psychologist-b-j-fogg.

2. Harness the power of accountability to increase your odds of success. Having a person or system to make you more accountable can keep you on track and reinforce the habits you've formed. This could be a coach, partner, or mastermind group. If you're meeting with a person, make sure it's someone who recharges you, not someone who makes you want to avoid the activity!

You might find that an app that gives you prompts or sends you reminders works for you. Whichever it is, be flexible, explore what suits you and your style, and realize that what works could change over time.

3. Practice the Friday 5 strategy. Consistency is important when implementing a new behavior, but it's easy to get distracted when, for example, a huge new project comes along. The Friday 5 strategy helps you stay on, or get back on, track.

The Friday 5 Strategy

The Friday 5 strategy was designed by Beth when she observed a pattern among her clients. These clients had many goals they wanted to accomplish but could not figure out a way to change their behaviors, whether physical, mental, or emotional. To help them establish positive and healthy habits, she developed the Friday 5 strategy for putting the Benatti Resiliency Model® into action with a weekly cue and steps to follow.

1. Start by opening your calendar and scheduling a five-minute Friday 5 strategy session. Schedule it as a repeating meeting for a specific period of time, like six months. By the way, you can schedule this exercise for any day of the week, but many people like doing it on Fridays because the stress of the week has lifted. What's important is the consistency.

2. In your strategy session, answer the following three questions. Consider writing down your answers for more impact.

   a. What were my resilience wins this week? Write down any wins, even if small. For example, if you wanted to hydrate more, and did, write that down.

   b. What is my resilience goal for next week? Set a goal tied to one of the five areas of the Benatti Resiliency

Model. Make it concrete and measurable. For example, if you've decided to learn a new language, your goal could be to check out three language-learning options.

c. What is my plan to achieve that goal? Having a goal is fine, but increase your odds of achieving it by making a plan. From the example above, you could put an appointment with yourself in your calendar to spend an hour exploring options.

3. On a daily basis, ask yourself, "What can I do today to boost my resilience?" Even if you skip the Friday 5 weekly session, doing something small every day will boost your resilience and taking small steps on a regular basis leads to confidence to achieve bigger goals.

To download a Friday 5 reminder, go to https:// bethkennedy.com/rethink-resilience-friday-5/.

I have learned during my coaching career that you can improve your resilience by focusing on new habits and making them stick for you.

—Beth Kennedy

KEEP
CALM
AND
BE
RESILIENT

About the Authors

Photo by Emily Cikanek

Whether it's leadership coaching, conducting training programs, or speaking at professional conferences and symposiums, Beth Benatti Kennedy's mission is to recharge individuals in their careers and lives so that they have the energy needed for a rapidly changing world and environment. She has more than twenty-five years of experience as a leadership and team coach, resiliency-training expert, and speaker. Her Benatti Resiliency Model® has helped thousands of people develop the resilience to adapt to changing career circumstances, remain productive and engaged, and find greater life and career satisfaction. Her diverse client list includes dozens of individuals, small businesses, and corporations such as Takeda Pharmaceuticals USA, The Gillette Company, Nautilus Biotechnology, Amtrak, and Pfizer.

As a leadership coach, Beth guides leaders to develop resilience habits to support peak performance, maximize their professional and personal impact, positively influence the people they work with, and build their brand. Her training programs focus on giving employees the tools to stay resilient, make sense of organization changes, and manage change and transition within the organization. As a motivator and speaker at conferences, seminars, and symposiums, Beth has presented the Benatti Resiliency Model across the globe, including at TEDxNortheasternU. In addition, because of her expertise in resilience and burnout, she has been quoted in articles, interviewed on podcasts, and contributed to various publications. She is the author of *Career ReCharge: Five Strategies to Boost Resilience and Beat Burnout.*

Beth serves as a board member of PathWise, a multifaceted career management company, and is a member of the Bethany College Alumni Council. She is a certified Executive and Leadership Development Coach and holds certifications as a 360Reach Analyst (personal brand assessment) and in the Leadership Circle Profile. Her expertise includes being qualified to administer the Myers-Briggs Type Indicator® instrument, TypeCoach resources, and the Thomas-Kilmann Conflict Mode Instrument. She holds a BS from Bethany College, West Virginia, an MS in Human Resource Counseling from Northeastern University, Boston, and a Certificate of Advanced Graduate Studies in Marriage and Family Therapy from the University of Massachusetts at Boston.

Beth enjoys owning her own business, Benatti Leadership Development, following in her dad's footsteps as an entrepreneur and using her maiden name, Benatti, as a way to honor her dad. She is devoted to her family, her community, and her dog, Maple, whose picture appears with Booster number 2! Key to her personal recharge are her practices of yoga and meditation, as well as traveling, spending time with friends, and exercise.

Karthik Venkatakrishnan is a clinical pharmacologist and drug development scientist engaged in pharmaceutical research and development (R&D). As Vice President and Global Head of Quantitative Pharmacology at EMD Serono Inc., Billerica, Massachusetts, he is accountable for leadership of Clinical Pharmacology, Translational Modeling and Simulation, and Pharmacometrics in support of global pharmaceutical R&D. Previously, Karthik held roles in Clinical Pharmacology at Pfizer Inc. and Takeda Pharmaceuticals, including as Head of Quantitative Clinical Pharmacology at Takeda Pharmaceuticals International Co., Cambridge, Massachusetts.

Karthik's areas of professional and research interest include oncology R&D, model-informed global drug development, and topics in translational science at the interface of drug metabolism and clinical pharmacology. Karthik received his PhD in Pharmacology and Experimental Therapeutics at Tufts University in Boston, Massachusetts. He is a Fellow of the American College of Clinical Pharmacology and a member of the American Society for Clinical Pharmacology and Therapeutics (ASCPT), having served as Chair of the ASCPT Scientific Program Committee (2013–2014) and Chair of the ASCPT Quantitative Pharmacology Network (2017–2018). He is an author of over one hundred seventy-five scientific publications and over fifty abstracts and a recipient of the ASCPT Clinical and Translational Science Award in 2018 and the ASCPT Malle Jurima-Romet Mid-Career Leadership Award in 2021. Karthik is an Associate Editor of *Clinical Pharmacology and Therapeutics* and a member of the Editorial Boards of *Clinical and Translational Science*, *The Journal of Clinical Pharmacology*, and *Clinical Pharmacology in Drug Development*.

Karthik is passionate about talent development, mentorship, and scientific writing. He believes in approaching scientific problem-solving and technical writing as a highly collaborative and artistic endeavor, akin to symphonic orchestration of music. In doing so, he enjoys engaging, learning from, co-creating with, enabling, and empowering people with diverse technical, professional, geographical, and cultural backgrounds, anchored by *purpose*, *trust*, and *gratitude* as foundational tenets for professional success and personal fulfillment.

Photo courtesy of ASCPT

Songmao (Ben) Zheng is a biopharmaceutical scientist. As Vice President, Head of Clinical and Quantitative Pharmacology at Adagene Inc., he leads model-informed drug discovery and development in both the preclinical and clinical space. Prior to this role, he was Scientific Director/Group Leader leading numerous biologics programs at Janssen BioTherapeutics, Janssen R&D. He has been extensively involved with preclinical, translational, and early clinical PK/TE/PD characterization and has provided scientific and strategic input for biologics across therapeutic areas.

Songmao obtained his BS degree in Biological Sciences from Sichuan University (University of Washington [UW] exchange program) in 2007, then a PhD degree in Pharmaceutical Sciences from UW in 2012, followed by his postdoctoral training at the Center for Pharmacometrics & Systems Pharmacology at the University of Florida (UF). He was an intern at Seattle Genetics in 2010 and an ORISE Fellow at the US Food and Drug Administration in 2013. Songmao has authored around thirty peer-reviewed publications (accumulative Impact Factor around 200), including book chapters, and presented in over thirty conferences with six awards. He is also the co-inventor for nine patents (some pending). Within the seven years he was with Janssen, he won one Philip B. Hofmann Research Scientist Award (the second-highest scientific recognition in Johnson & Johnson [J&J]), two J&J Leadership Awards, one Janssen Innovation Leadership Award, and about twenty-five J&J ENCORE/Inspire awards. Songmao is an Editorial Board member for the American Society for Clinical Pharmacology and Therapeutics' (ASCPT) Family Journals *Clinical Pharmacology & Therapeutics* and *Clinical and Translational Science*. He was also a member of the Scientific Program Committee of ASCPT (2021–2024), and is an Affiliate Associate Professor at UW and Courtesy Adjunct Assistant Professor at UF.

Songmao was born in Chongqing, China, and is passionate about art, science, humanity, and nature in general. Besides his landscape photography trips to over twenty-five US National Parks/Monuments/Forests, he has worked with over two hundred models as a portrait photographer, besides mathematical models! Last but not least, Songmao has evolved to become a tropical plant and orchid collector, and has constructed a semiautomatic growing system in his all-season greenhouse in Hardiness zone 6b with over one thousand plants.